The Wall St. Panic of 2008: If you lost money, here's why.

By William Thayer

Table of Contents

Why this book was written

In September 2008, Lehman Brothers declared bankruptcy, AIG was bailed out with $85 Billion of taxpayer money, and Wall St. panicked. Overnight lending froze up, and it appeared possible that our economy could be headed for another Great Depression. In the ensuing weeks, Congress passed an enormous bailout bill of $700 Billion known as TARP. This lessened the chances of a Depression, but the stock market eventually dropped approximately 50% which decimated millions of 401 (k) retirement plans for most Americans.

The explanation given for this crisis was that it was all due to Subprime Mortgages. While Subprimes played an important role, the roots of the Wall St. Crash are deeper than that. For example, one of the critical causes of the Lehman bankruptcy was its excessive leverage of 40 to 1 and massive overnight lending. This is hardly discussed today, and no corrective action has taken place even though more than 1 year has passed. Someone has to say something even if that someone is me. This is the first reason why this book has been written.

When I tried to explain to my sons (one has an MS in Biology and the other a BS in Biology) why a Balance Sheet should never have 40 to 1 leverage, they asked me what a Balance Sheet was. I realized I had a problem. They and many Americans do not know what a Balance Sheet is, what an Opaque Derivative is or what Credit Default Swaps are? If you don't understand these concepts, you can't possibly understand why we had the Wall St. Panic of 2008 or why it can happen again. This is the second reason why this book was written. This book will give a simplified explanation of these key concepts.

A third reason why this book has been written is that Wall St. seems to have largely forgotten what the essence of capitalism is. Capital investment has been critical for the development of our railroads, planes and computers. However, instead of channeling money into such useful investments which build our economy and create jobs, Wall St. has been putting a tremendous amount of money into non productive junk – make believe insurance called Credit Default Swaps and useless Derivatives[1]. Wall St. needs a good slap in the face, and that is the third reason for this book. Wall St.'s criteria seem to be: (1) Can I make money, and (2) Can I do it legally. These are good enough criteria for Las Vegas but not Wall St. Wall St. needs to return to its old criteria of: (3) Can I create growth/jobs and (4) Can I improve productivity.

No one (Congress, Wall St., Regulators, and Accounting Boards) seems to know what to do to prevent another similar crash. To help end this intellectual paralysis, this book will list a number of specific recommendations. That is the final reason for this book.

---

[1] not all Derivatives are useless

Part 1. Introduction

This Part begins with an executive summary of the entire book. Following that, I introduce my mode of thinking (e.g., Input $\rightarrow$ System $\rightarrow$ Output) which may not be the standard approach in financial books. Next, a short review of why capitalism is the best system is made. However, the excessive leverage, Opaque Derivatives and Credit Default Swaps described in Part 2 have nothing to do with good capitalism. In order to understand these concepts, it is necessary to first understand the Balance Sheet, and a short history of its origin is given. Also, in order to understand the Wall St. Panic, it is necessary to have some idea of the various parameters in our financial system from our GDP to the size of the Subprime Losses. A basic reference table is provided.

2

Chapter 1. Executive Summary

This book is divided into three Parts. The thesis of this book is that the faulty Wall St. System crashed when it received a Bad Input (Subprime Mortgages). At a top level, the Wall St. System is faulty due to three primary reasons:

Financial Cause (1): Balance Sheet Abuse
Financial Cause (2): Opaque Derivatives
Financial Cause (3): Credit Default Swaps.

Part 1. Introduction
The purpose of this Part is to lay the foundations for a good understanding of Part 2 which is the heart of the book. Two key areas are addressed. The first is the Balance Sheet. If you do not understand the Balance Sheet, you cannot understand why Bear Stearns and Lehman failed. The second area is a Fact Table of the key parameters necessary for an understanding of our financial system. It is necessary to have a general grasp of the system in order to put the discussion of this book in context.

Part 2. Why Wall St. Panicked
At a top level, there were four key elements involved in the Wall St. Panic – Subprimes, Balance Sheet Abuse, Opaque Derivatives and Credit Defaults Swaps. At this point, if you are like my sons, you may not know what these terms even mean. By the end of this Part, you should have a fair idea. You may not end up an expert, but your knowledge will be better than most in America. For those desiring more knowledge, I supply plenty of Wikipedia references and an extensive bibliography. Hopefully for many, this book will just be a start. This is a critical area for American citizens to understand. The Wall St. Panic has

affected our economic growth, our unemployment level, our retirement plans and much more.

Part 3. Why Wall St. will Panic again

The simple answer of why Wall St. will Panic again is that no fundamental reforms have been made. First, I talk about what the Fed actually did in response to the Panic. Next, I briefly discuss the failures of the Fed, Government Regulators and Self Regulators. Finally, I make specific Recommendations on what should be done. At the time of this writing, the Dodd Bill is being discussed in Congress. The final product is, at this time, unknown. Although the Dodd Bill has many flaws, it is better than nothing which is what we have now. I compare the Dodd Bill to my Recommendations and show that except for the Volcker Rule, it basically falls short.

In the past, Wall St. financed the growth in our economy. In short, it added value. It still does that to a degree, but it has put a tremendous amount of money and effort into useless, dangerous products of creative finance including Opaque Derivatives, Synthetic Derivatives and Credit Default Swaps. Wall St. needs to get back On-Track and concentrate on adding value.

Chapter 2. Introduction

Exec Summary: This chapter will introduce my mode of thinking.

Don't Trust Me

This book will present my view of what caused the Wall St. Panic. However, I encourage every reader to do their own research and analysis. There is an extensive bibliography at the end of this book. In the computer age, it is easier and cheaper to get another view on the subjects I am addressing. My first recommendation is to go to Wikipedia and second to do a google search. In the Bibliography, I list a number of good websites and books to help with your own research and analysis. I will give Wikipedia references throughout this book.

My recommendation on how to read this book

My goal is to get across general concepts and not precise knowledge. This is not an academic book. There is no test at the end of this book. If you walk away with more knowledge (not necessarily all the concepts I discuss), my goal has been achieved. This is best done by simply reading straight through the book (about 2 to 3 hours). Although there are numbers in the text, I have tried to push most numbers and more advanced discussion to the Appendices or Chapter Notes. Finance has its own set of vocabulary and acronyms which I have placed a Glossary at the very rear of the book for easy access. Also, the Fact Table for financial parameters is at the rear of the book.

References [2-1]

I am not going to be meticulous about references (remember, this is not an academic book). I don't randomly pluck my numbers from thin air. I get them from a variety of financial sources [2-1] and sometimes interpolate for the numbers I need. For example, if you do a google search for the size of the CDS market, you will find that the numbers are all over the place. I can get answers that range from $15 to $60 Trillion. Therefore I select a weighted average depending on credibility (obviously a judgment).

My Background

The backgrounds of most of the authors in the Bibliography are journalists/writers along with a few people from the financial industry and academia. Is my background any better than theirs? I'm certainly not going to claim that, but my background is certainly different. I'm just an Average Joe from Main Street.

I earned a BS in Math from Stanford. At USC, I earned a Master's in Aerospace Engineering and a Master's in Business Administration. Although most of my approximately 30 years in the aerospace industry were spent in engineering, I did spend two years in finance/accounting for the Hughes Satellite Division. In 1992, as a result of our success in the Cold War, I was laid off as an engineer and found out what it is like to be unemployed. I know firsthand what it feels like to have to pay for your mortgage, food, health insurance when you have no income and two young kids. I have a lot of empathy for the millions of Americans that have lost their jobs as a result of the Wall St. Panic. After being turned down for approximately 100 jobs in engineering and business, I finally discovered that I was self employed whether I liked it or not. I tried everything. I earned my stock broker licenses, the NASD Series 7 & 63. I earned my IRS Enrolled Agent designation which allowed me to prepare taxes and represent taxpayers before the IRS. After a two year effort, I earned my designation as a Certified Financial Planner (a very worthwhile effort). Finally, I earned my California Real Estate License. My success was as a Real Estate Agent in Manhattan Beach, CA although I did also work as a Financial Planner for 14 years.

Quite by accident, I gained all the background to understand the elements that went into the Subprime meltdown which in turn led to the Wall St. Panic. Again, my understanding does not come from academia or government experience. It comes from being down in the trenches where people actually have to work for a living. I understand mortgage applications quite well. I have a good understanding of the Southern California real estate market which was one of the epicenters of the real estate meltdown. I understand accounting since I had to prepare a dozen financial statements every year I was a Registered Investment Adviser. These accounting statements were routinely audited by representatives from the California Department of Corporations (and they sure did a better job than the SEC did auditing Madoff). I understand the stock brokerage business since I worked as one.

Am I unqualified to write this book?
No. Some of the billionaire bankers of Wall St. didn't even graduate from college let alone earn an MBA. The well paid executives of Bear Stearns and Lehman Brothers ran those companies with leverage of 40 to 1. A "D" student going for his MBA could do better than that. A beginning accountant could have figured out that AIG's Credit Default Swaps were simply an empty promise. I could run a business more ethically than that. The Fed let Lehman fail for the same reasons as Bear failed. Every engineer knows that you have to do a failure analysis and feed the results back into the system. No, with the colossal stupidity shown at so many levels of the Wall St. Panic, I don't feel unqualified at all.

Scope of this book – "Magic + 1"
In the Chapter 1 Executive Summary, I briefly stated the thesis of this book:

The Wall St. Financial System was faulty for three primary reasons: (1) Balance Sheet Abuse, (2) Opaque Derivatives and (3) Credit Default Swaps. A Bad Input, Subprime Mortgages, caused Panic and brought the system down.

Is the explanation for the Wall St. Panic really that simple? Of course not. It's much more complicated [2-2]. However, to keep this book as simplified as possible, I will just concentrate on those four elements. In Part 3, I will discuss why I think a future Panic is possible and introduce another potential cause – Hedge Funds.

The level of explanation in this book is what I describe as "Magic + 1". Here is the story behind that term.

Magic, Magic +1 and Magic + 2
An aircraft engineer was on a remote Pacific Island talking to an aborigine when an airplane flew overhead. The aborigine asked the engineer to explain how it was possible for the plane to fly. The engineer wrote down the Lift Equation. That was too complicated for the aborigine. He said, "I don't understand it." Then the engineer tried to explain it without equations by verbally describing the partial pressure on the upper surface of the wing. No luck. The aborigine again said, "I don't understand it". Finally, in exasperation, the engineer simply said, "It's Magic." The aborigine smiled and said, "Ah Magic. That I understand."

The explanation of the Wall St. Panic which simply describes it as "The Subprime Mess" is the "Magic" level of description. This book which concentrates on four key elements is the "Magic + 1" level of description. A book that included the top 20 elements could be classed as a "Magic + 2" level (and I haven't seen one of those books).

Mode of Thinking I – Ball Park Thinking

I am going to make several assertions in this book. For example, I will assert that the Subprime problem was not large enough to have caused the size of the Wall St. Panic. Well, a first question would be, "How do I know what the size of the Subprime problem was?" I don't know exactly, but using available data, I can make an informed estimate. I describe this as "Ball Park Thinking". It could also be described as a "Back of the Envelope" calculation. The point is not to focus on a precise answer but just one that is close (or in the Ball Park). Let me illustrate this with a story from my Quantum Mechanics Professor at Stanford.

How many barbers in the USA?

When my Professor went to his Oral Exam for his PhD in Physics, he wasn't quite ready for the first question he was asked:

How many barbers are there in the USA?

At first, he wondered if he was in the wrong room. Was this the committee for an Economic PhD? Then, after, recovering from his initial shock, he realized that what they were really asking him was to **_think_**. What assumptions could he make? What deductions could he make? He started to speak. He said that he had his hair cut every month. It took the barber about 15 minutes to cut his hair (crew cut). His barber worked 40 hours/week, and he always had customers waiting for their turn. He did a little mental math and came up with a number of how many men his barber could cut hair for in a year. Then he estimated how many men there were in the USA. Dividing this number by his barber's production rate gave him an estimate for the number of barbers in the USA. Was his number precisely correct? Even the committee didn't know. What they were interested in was his "Ball Park Thinking".

This is the type of thinking that will be used in this book. Precision numbers are not the goal. Good, fearless thinking is.

Mode of Thinking II – Pilot Thinking

In addition to being an aircraft design and flight test engineer, I was a private pilot. There is a different type of thinking required if you are a pilot. You have to solve the problem that you are faced with not the problem you choose to solve. Furthermore, you have to solve the problem with the best information you have at the time. You don't have the luxury of waiting to acquire perfect and complete information. In fact, much critical data on the Wall St. Panic is being kept deliberately secret by our government as well as the financial industry [2-3]. Despite this, an analysis should be done.

This Pilot Thinking is in complete contrast to the type of thinking of an academic economist. If the economist is not ready to put forward his solution to a particular problem, he can just put it off until next Monday. Try that with a failed engine. Or, if an economist doesn't like the problem he is working on, he can just choose another. Well, the failed engine problem chooses you [2-4].

What I am saying is that in analyzing the Wall St. Panic, it is necessary to address the important elements that contributed to it even if our knowledge of these elements is incomplete. For example, I identify Credit Default Swaps as Financial Cause (3). Has anyone written a book about them? Has the financial media analyzed the Credit Default Swap (CDS) problem? No. This book will. It will do so not because I have complete knowledge (which I certainly don't), but because it is an important and necessary problem to analyze and solve. I don't choose to analyze CDS. It chose me.

Miracle on the Hudson
Probably everyone knows the story of the Miracle on the Hudson. A US Airways plane took off from LaGuardia and big Canadian geese were ingested into both engines which caused them to fail shortly thereafter. The pilot didn't choose to have a failed engines problem, but he had to solve it. With both engines gone, his plane acquired the aerodynamic characteristics of a rock. He knew he didn't have a lot of time to assess his data and make a decision. He knew he couldn't make it back to LaGuardia Airport (Plan A) or over to Teterboro Airport (Plan B) so he made a magnificent landing in the Hudson River (Plan C).

Mode of Thinking III – The Black Box [2]
When I worked on satellites, I had to become an electrical engineer whether I liked it or not. The circuitry that goes into a communications satellite is mind boggling. A single engineer can only understand a small portion. However, it is necessary to have an overall understanding of the complete satellite. In order to do this, the description of the satellite design is simplified by lumping circuitry into a series of different black boxes. In fact, this is usually how the satellite is manufactured.

The concept of black box thinking is that you have a system (the black box). From the left, the black box receives an input. Going out the right side of the black box

---

[2] Not the Black Box retrieved from an airplane crash

is the output. Let me illustrate this with a couple of simple examples:

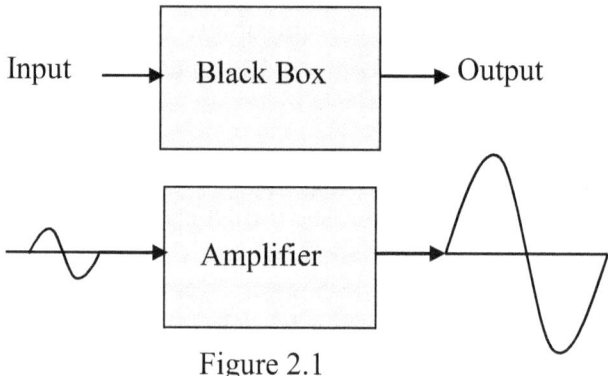

Figure 2.1

In Figure 2.1, a small sine wave is the Input, and a large sine wave is the Output. The Black Box (an Amplifier) has magnified the Input wave. I visualize the Wall St. Panic in a similar manner. In my opinion, what we should have had as a result from the Subprime Meltdown was an ordinary Recession. Instead what we had was a Panic, and the worst financial crisis since the Great Depression.

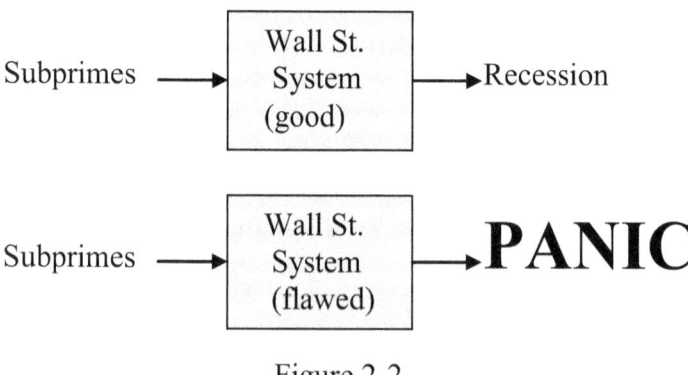

Figure 2-2

If our Wall St. System was good, we would have had just a Recession. Since our present Wall St. System is flawed, we had a Panic. In the world of engineering, if a Black

Box System gives you a bad result, then the solution is pretty simple. You have to change the System. That's the thesis of this book. We need to correct Financial Causes (1), (2) and (3). I'm not advocating getting rid of Wall St. I'm just advocating changing it back to when it was operating better.

What about the Bad Input (Subprimes)? Well, we certainly need to correct that too. But my point is this:

The Subprimes were only an "Input". The more significant problem is a poor financial "System".

Why is a flawed financial system on Wall St. a major concern? If the Wall St. System receives a different "Bad Input", it will probably fail again. There are plenty of potential "Bad Inputs" out there. Please read Appendix 10. "Black Swans and Bad Inputs".

Summary
Ball Park, Pilot and Box Black [2-6] Thinking. You can tell already that this is not going to be your average financial book. You can also look forward to learning about "The Bolivian Method" and "Failure Investigations". Neither Wall St. nor the Subprimes are going to avoid a little scrutiny under the spotlight of some engineering analysis.

Addendum

Condescension
In her review of this book, my wife noted that I write in a condescending manner. This is true. When I write about the morons on Wall St. that brought us Opaque Derivatives and Credit Default Swaps or inadequately capitalized Balance Sheets, this condescension is entirely intentional. When I try to explain to the reader what a mortgage and a Balance Sheet are, this will seem elementary to an MBA or CPA. To them it might seem condescending. That's not the

intent. My goal is to reach as many Americans as I can such as my sons. They're smart, but they have no idea what a mortgage is, what a Balance Sheet is, let alone Derivatives or Credit Default Swaps.

Clarity
This book is going to violate most rules for good writing in the name of trying to be as clear as possible. Therefore, I may capitalize words when that is not strictly allowed. I will put words or sentences in bold, italicized print to emphasis their importance. Since Finance is a tough subject, I will put definitions in boxes as well as define words in the Glossary at the end of the book. The end result of this book is not to win a Pulitzer Prize for good writing. If I could win a prize for clarity, I would be satisfied.

Chapter 3. Capitalism is Best

Exec Summary: This chapter compares capitalism to communism and welfare states.

This book is going to criticize many of the abusive financial activities of Wall St. banks. Does this mean I am against banks or capitalism? Absolutely not. The banking activity is crucial to supplying the capital we need for our businesses to grow. However, when banks start creating Opaque Derivatives, they are doing us a disservice and abusing capitalism. Capitalism is the best economic system on the face of the earth. This is not to say that capitalism is perfect. It is just a whole lot better than the alternatives of communism, socialism or the welfare state.

Communism vs. Capitalism

Let's compare Russian Communism with American Free Enterprise. When the Cold War ended, it was pretty obvious which system worked better. The US economy was 10 times the size of the Russian economy and they had more people.

When I traveled to Russia in 1972, one of the prominent Russian economists spoke to our tour groups extolling the glories of communism. When I asked him when the communists expected to surpass the USA in economic power, he dodged the question. He said that if Russia hadn't suffered so severely in World War II (WWII), it would have past the USA by 1972. Certainly the western half of Russia was flattened in WWII, but Japan was 100% flattened. If the WWII damage argument was valid, then Japan shouldn't have surpassed the Soviet Union to become the number 2 economic power when they had only 1/3 of the population of the Soviet Union. Or, let's take the case of East and West Germany. Both were equally flattened in

WWII. When Germany was reunited, it was pretty obvious which economic system was better. Sorry Comrade, it's the system.

If we need any more confirmation, we need only look at China. Now China has kept the communist one party government, but it has turned most of its economy loose on capitalism since 1980. The result is that they have grown at 10% a year for nearly 30 years. This means their economy has doubled every 7 years or grown an astounding 16 fold in that period. Contrast this growth with the 30 years that Mao was in charge of their economic system from 1950-1980. Which system worked better for the Chinese?

One Secret of Capitalism – Bottom up

Now that the Cold War is over, I will let the Russians in on one reason why our system blitzed theirs. The Communist System was an economy planned from the top down. At the top was the 5 Year Planning Commission (Gosplan). This worked fairly well when you were planning how much coal each steel plant needed, but it was a little weak on *INNOVATION*. By contrast, our capitalist system is largely from the bottom up.

Let me illustrate this with a story told to me by my Dad. He was selected as one of General Electric's promising young engineers and sent to its finishing school at Schnectady, New York. In his class of 1938, there was another promising young engineer named David Packard. He decided to leave GE after the class and started a company in his Palo Alto garage with another engineer named Hewlett. Their company is known today as Hewlett Packard or HP. This company was not the result of top down planning, but rather bottom up planning. Sorry Comrade.

While on the subject of Palo Alto garages, it might be worthwhile to recall another bottom up story. Steve Jobs and his buddy Steve Wozniak started their company, Apple Computer, in a garage not too far away from Packard's garage.

What was the Russian problem? Did they have too few garages? No, they had top down planning. If you want the Post Office running our economy, then top down government planning is the best choice. If you want bottom up planning (as in Packard, Jobs, Edison), then our capitalist system is best.

Today we have the government involved in the running of General Motors. Does anyone want to bet that GM will do better than Ford in the next few years?

Capitalism vs. Euro Welfare States

Let's compare our Capitalist system with the Welfare States of Europe. Those Welfare States are not like Communism. The government controls about half the economy vs. the approximately 20% that our government controls (although that percentage is getting bigger due to the Panic and Big Government). If you want to start a business in a Welfare State, it is tough. You are blitzed with stifling bureaucratic rules. You can't just lay off someone if your business contracts. You have to protect their job whether it makes economic sense or not. The result is that few people want to start a business even if they have a garage. You have to think real hard about hiring someone if you know you can't lay them off. This means less *INNOVATION.*

The development of the personal computer is an example. Why wasn't it developed in Europe? It is because the bureaucratic barriers to entry make it difficult to start any new business there. When was the last time you saw a computer laptop that was made in France?

Now am I saying that the Europeans are stupid? Hardly. They have brilliant scientists like Tim Berners-Lee who contributed to the internet. He did this while working as a scientist at CERN, one of the world's best nuclear particle research facilities. But did the internet start in Europe? No. It started in Silicon Valley. Why? One reason is that the software engineers of Netscape worked 90 hours a week to make it happen. Contrast that to France where the 35 hour week is golden.

Greek Welfare State Crisis

The current Greek Economic Crisis illustrates the flaws of the Welfare State. They promise too much, work too little and innovate hardly at all. Eventually the promises cannot be met, and the result for Greece will probably be a debt default.

The bottom line is that our system is the best and most productive. It certainly isn't perfect, but it is way ahead of whatever is in second place.

Pie Dividers and Pie Makers

My wife is a TV food network junkie so I explained the difference between socialism/welfare state and capitalism in terms of pies. The overarching aim of socialism is to "divide the pie" as equally as possible. Germany is an example. They have only 60,000 millionaires and no one as rich as Bill Gates or Michael Dell. Here's the downside to their approach. They don't have any Microsoft or Dell Computer either. When Bill Gates and Michael Dell came to America's capitalism party, they brought their own pies. They added to America's pie supply. If they get a larger piece, I don't mind. They added value. The emphasis of capitalism is fundamentally different than socialism. Its emphasis is on "pie building".

Capitalism can get off the tracks

I maintain that capitalism is the best system, but I will also say that it can get off the tracks. It needs constant monitoring and correction to be at its most efficient. The essence of capitalism is freedom. The downside of this is that people/companies/banks have the freedom to abuse the system or decrease its efficiency, productivity or innovation. Here are some examples:

The 1929 Great Depression

While the causes of the Great Depression are still debated, there is no question that one of the greatest contributing factors was excessive leverage. For example, an individual investor could buy stock with just 5% of his own money and 95% borrowed from the stock brokerage on margin. This was a great advantage when the market was going up, but it was a disaster when the market went down. When the market initially dropped 5% in 1929, many investors were completely wiped out. Their failure cascaded into brokerage and bank failures. In a very short time, this was translated into 10 years of economic stagnation.

Was it a great idea to let individual investors buy stocks with just 5% down? Obviously not. The government responded by issuing a new rule that investors had to put down a minimum of 50% of their own money to purchase a stock, and this removed one of the factors of the Great Depression. In other words, some limited and smart intervention by the government is necessary. Complete laissez-faire is dangerous. The eternal issue is to come up with limited, intelligent regulation that will ensure a safe, fair and efficient system and not slow down growth.

In the last Part of this book, I will briefly discuss how Hedge Funds, including LTCM, have essentially found a way around the 50% down rule. Before, its bailout in 1998, LTCM had only put 1% down. LTCM is just one example of Hedge Fund abuse. The 10% drop in the stock market on May 6, 2010 is another.

Rockefeller Oil Monopoly of 1900
The world's oil industry started in the United States. By 1900, Rockefeller had nearly a complete monopoly of the oil business. This was an abuse of the freedom of capitalism and laissez-faire. Monopolies aren't efficient or fair. An Oil Monopoly could charge any price it wanted for oil. The government intervened and broke up the monopoly. Competition between oil companies was restored.

ATT Phone Monopoly
Once when I was a student at Stanford in the 1960s, I had a spirited discussion with another Math major who was a confirmed Socialist. While I was arguing that competition was always best, he was for total government ownership. He did stump me with his argument for one current monopoly that he thought should be owned by the government – the ATT Phone Monopoly. He argued that it would be stupid to build two sets of telephone poles etc. At the time, I couldn't come up with an effective counter argument, but look at the situation today. The government broke up the ATT Phone Monopoly, and the result has been nothing but remarkable innovation and lower costs. Would ATT of the 1960s ever have wanted to develop cell phones when it had a complete monopoly on landline phones? Would ATT have developed a Blackberry? Probably not.

Capitalism On-Track and Off-Track

Figure 1.1

When Wall St. went off track in 1929, it dragged the economy down as well. The same was true in 2008.

When a Wall St. bank lends money to General Electric to build new jet engines or Ford to build new cars, these are examples of Capitalism being On-Track. These loans lead to new products, more jobs and greater GDP. However, when Wall St. banks create complex, Opaque Derivatives or issue Credit Default Swaps (CDS), these are examples of Capitalism getting Off-Track. These Derivatives and CDS create no new products, no new jobs and do not increase our GDP. What they do is create huge bonuses for Wall St. and huge risk in our financial system. The focus of this book is on describing how Wall St. got Off-Track. The author has no problem with a Wall St. that is On-Track.

Summary

I'm all for capitalism, but I do recognize the need for limited, intelligent government regulation in the financial and business sectors. We want a free market, but we do not want an irresponsible market. The above examples illustrate some reasons why. Special interests on Wall St. are arguing against regulation and disclosure of Derivatives, Credit Default Swaps and Hedge Funds. I am in total disagreement with these positions and will explain why later in this book.

Capitalism is our best economic tool, but we must be careful that it is not abused. The Great Depression of 1929 and the Panic of 2008 show that capitalism can be abused. We need to get our system back On-Track.

Chapter 4. Fact Table

Exec Summary: To understand the Wall St. Panic, it is necessary to know the sizes of the financial elements of our economic system such as Subprime mortgage market, bank capital and more. This info is presented in a Fact Table in this Chapter and at the end of the book.

> ### What a Stanford PhD didn't know
> On a recent cruise to Antarctica, I was discussing this book with a fellow passenger, a Stanford PhD. I said that the $600 Trillion Derivative market is huge compared to our yearly GDP. The GDP, of course, is how much 300 million Americans make each year. He gave me a blank look. I asked if he had any idea how big our GDP was? He took a wild guess of $1 Trillion. Wow. This doesn't say much about a Stanford education since our GDP is $14 Trillion. Fortunately, his PhD was in geology not economics. Nevertheless this incident highlighted to me the importance of describing the sizes of the financial elements that have a bearing on the Wall St. Panic.

Personal Wealth as an example
As a Financial Planner, when I first met with a new client my first task was to understand his current financial position. A first question would be to determine how much he made each year. Let's say $70,000/year. A second question would be to determine his net worth or capital (as on a Balance Sheet). Let me assume that this person has a $300,000 house with a mortgage of $200,000. His net worth in the house is the difference or $100,000. Let me assume that he also has $50,000 in the stock market (e.g., a retirement account). Now I can start building a financial picture of this individual as shown below. On the right side of the Table, I show the national financial parameters that correspond to this person's data.

My Client		USA
Yearly Income:	$70,000	GDP
Wealth:		
House Market Value:	$300,000	Total Real Estate Value
- House Mortgage:	$200,000	-Total Mortgage Value
House Capital	$100,000	Total Real Estate Capital
Stock Market	$ 50,000	Stock Market Value
Total Wealth:	$150,000	National Wealth [4-1]

Table 4.1

Now in Table 4.1, I merely added my client's House Capital ($100,000) to his Stock Market ($50,000) to determine his total wealth. For the National Wealth of the USA, it is more complicated. For this book, however, I will just concentrate on three elements: Real Estate Value, Stock Market Value and all Other (not shown above).

Fact Table of National Financial Elements
A Ball Park estimate of the financial elements of our national economy that are relevant to the discussion in this book are given in Table 4.2 below. Let me discuss each section.

I. GDP
This is our Gross Domestic Product which represents the yearly production of all 300 million Americans. The GDP dropped a few percent as a result of the Panic, but basically remained the same at $14 Trillion.

Fact Table of Financial Elements (In $Trillions)		
Element	Value before Panic	Value after Panic
I. GDP	14	14
II. National Wealth:		
Stock Market	10	5
Total Real Estate	15	12
Other [4-1]	39	33
National Wealth	64	50
III. Real Estate:		
Total Real Estate Value	15	12
Total Mortgages	10	10
Total Equity (Capital)	5	2
IV. Miscellaneous:		
Subprime Mortgages	2	1.6
Bank Capital	0.8	0.6
TARP		0.7
Stimulus Bill		0.8
V. Size of Derivative Market:		
Total Derivatives	600	599
Total CDS	30	30

Table 4.2

II. National Wealth

Our national wealth took a real hit as a result of the Panic. Our stock market dropped by 50% which meant investors and retirement funds took a $5 Trillion loss. Our real estate dropped in value by 20% or $3 Trillion. All other elements of our national wealth dropped approximately $6 Trillion for a total loss of $14 Trillion. That is 14 trillion reasons why you should be reading this book.

III. Real Estate

Nationally, our real estate value dropped from $15 to $12 Trillion. However, the mortgage value remained the same at $10 Trillion. This meant that our equity in our property shrank from $5 Trillion to $2 Trillion.

IV. Miscellaneous

The purpose of this section is to relate the size of the Subprime Loss to the Capital of Wall St. Banks, the TARP Rescue Package and the Job Stimulus Bill. It is pretty obvious that the $400 Billion Subprime Loss ($2 Trillion - $1.6 Trillion = $0.4 Trillion) is much smaller than either the TARP or Stimulus packages. Why? We had a Panic which is the focus of the discussion of this book.

V. Size of Derivative Market

Our GDP is $14 Trillion yet we have a $600 Trillion Derivative market with $30 Trillion of CDS. Does this make sense? No, it doesn't, and this book will explain why.

Now many of the financial elements that I have described including Subprimes, Derivatives, CDS and others may not be familiar to you at this point. Don't worry. The rest of this book is dedicated to explaining them.

Summary

The purpose of this Fact Table is just to provide a convenient reference for you as you read the book. A copy of this Fact Table is located on the last page of this book for easy access. Any parameters you don't understand at this point should become clearer as you read this book.

.

Chapter 5. Origins of Accounting

Exec Summary: The basic principles of the Balance Sheet are discussed.

Why should you care about Accounting?

In order to understand Financial Cause (1) Balance Sheet Abuse, you must first understand what a Balance Sheet is. That's not simple. What accountants have done is taken the simple Subtraction Equation and mangled it beyond all recognition.

According to the best records available from the San Diego Chapter of the Society for Mathematical Purity, the assault on the Subtraction Equation took place some 500 years ago in Venice, Italy. A man named Guido was studying mathematics, but found it too difficult and dropped out after learning about addition and subtraction. Dropping out at the Subtraction level is not too far along, but Guido was no ordinary dropout. He had a gift for marketing. He realized that if he gave the mathematical numbers different names and moved them around, he could create a whole new field which he called accounting. He started out a little slow with the Income Statement, but he picked up speed with the Balance Sheet. Let me tell the story.

Income Statement

Guido realized that businessmen (one step lower than a math dropout) had trouble figuring out how much money they were making or losing in their business or their bank. Since the only thing he knew was the Subtraction equation, he tried to apply it to their problem. Now the Subtraction Equation is shown below with some sample numbers to the right.

Subtraction Equation	
Number	10
- Other Number	- 8
Answer	2

Figure 5.1

Now Guido, realizing the mathematicians have zero marketing skills, took this innocent equation and renamed the elements and called it the Income Statement (vs. the Subtraction Equation) as shown below:

Income Statement	
Sales Revenue	10
- Expenses	- 8
Net Income (Answer)	2

Figure 5.2

The item of interest for the businessmen was the Answer or to use Guido's new term, Net Income. Since Net Income was on the last line, it became known as the Bottomline. This was an immediate hit with the businessmen of Venice, and Guido was making plenty of money as a Certified Public Accountant (CPA) until the businessmen realized that they could hire a poorly paid mathematician to do the same calculation. Guido was in trouble, but he was resourceful and came up with the Balance Sheet.

Balance Sheet
Sure, his Income Statement helped businessmen figure out if they were making or losing money in a given year, but how was their business overall? Guido immediately saw that his one math trick, the Subtraction Equation, could

answer this question as well. Again, he took the Subtraction Equation and renamed the elements. The result is shown below with some sample numbers.

Guido's Vertical Balance Sheet	
Assets	10
- Debt	- 8
Capital (Answer)	2

Figure 5.3

However, before he went public with his new Balance Sheet concept, Guido thought about how he could cut the low paid mathematicians out of the market. His stroke of genius was to make the Balance Sheet not resemble the Subtraction Equation at all. His first step was to move the elements out of a vertical column. This is shown in Figure 5.4 below. Please compare it to Figure 5.3

First step in the evolution of Guido's New Balance Sheet		
	Balance Sheet	
Assets 10		Debt -8
		Capital 2

Figure 5.4

Now already, he had confused the mathematicians who are used to seeing the Subtraction Equation as a vertical set of numbers. Secondly, he dropped the minus sign for the Debt. This was the nail in the coffin for the mathematicians. How could you have a Subtraction Equation without a minus sign? Now he didn't want to stray too far from a mathematics feel, so he next put a line under each of the two columns and added them up.

Second step in the evolution of Guido's New Balance Sheet			
	Balance Sheet		
Assets	10	Debt	8
		Capital	2
Total	10	Total	10

Figure 5.5

They were "in balance". Bingo! He called his new invention the "Balance Sheet". Talk about great marketing.

Guido had learned from his straightforward Income Statement that just looked like a Subtraction Equation. Sure, the Balance Sheet was just the same old Subtraction Equation, but Guido had learned from his brother, Luigi the Magician, to use guile and deception. First, he used no minus sign for Debt (even though he used it in his head to calculate Capital). Second, he didn't put the Answer (Capital) on the bottomline. These two clever moves have kept mathematicians from doing accounting for the past 5 centuries.

Summary
The Balance Sheet is not scary or mysterious. It is just the Subtraction Equation in a different format.

Addendum

Capitalization Rate and Leverage

Now in the centuries after "Guido the Subtractor", accountants moved up the mathematics chain to multiplication and division. We are just concerned with a couple of their division calculations in this book.

Definition: Leverage

If the Asset value is divided by the Capital, this is called Leverage. In Figure 5.5, Assets = 10 and Capital = 2. Therefore the Leverage is: 10/2 = 5.

Definition: Capitalization Rate

If the Capital is divided by the Assets, this is called the Capitalization Rate. In Figure 5.5, Assets = 10 and Capital = 2. Therefore, the Capitalization Rate is 2/10 = 0.2 or 20%. The Fed required normal banks to have an 8% Capitalization Rate whereas the SEC required only 2% for investment banks.

Summary of Part 1. Introduction

The purpose of Part 1. has been to lay out a roadmap for the rest of the book, and provide some background information for the discussion in Part 2. Causes of the Wall St. Panic.

The thesis of this book is that Wall St. panicked because of a Bad Input and 3 Financial Causes:

Bad Input: Subprime Mortgages
Financial Cause (1): Balance Sheet Abuse (Leverage)
Financial Cause (2): Derivatives
Financial Cause (3): Credit Default Swaps (CDS)

It is nearly impossible to understand the Bad Input or Financial Cause (1) without understanding the concept of the Balance Sheet. As Chapter 5 has shown, the Balance Sheet is nothing more than the Subtraction Equation in a mangled format.

Finally, this book is not about bashing capitalism or banks that do true investing or capital allocation. These banks have my full support. This book is about the financial causes of the Wall St. Panic which have nothing at all to do with good capitalism.

Part 2. Causes of the Wall St. Panic

This Part discusses the three major causes of the flawed Wall St. System:

Financial Cause (1) Balance Sheet Abuse
Financial Cause (2) Opaque Derivatives
Financial Cause (3) Credit Default Swaps (CDS)

A flawed system will not necessarily fail unless it receives a Bad Input. The Bad Input that the Wall St. System received was Subprime Mortgages. At the end of this Part, the reader should have a good idea of what Subprimes, Balance Sheet Abuse (or Excessive Leverage), Opaque Derivatives and Credit Default Swaps mean.

Chapter 6. Bad Input: Subprimes

Exec Summary: **This chapter will discuss the characteristics of Subprimes, NINJA loans, teaser rates, reset point and the role of Congress.**

The Subprime Crisis

The Wall St. Crash of 2008 has been described by many as The Subprime Crisis. Is this true? It is partially true. The Subprimes were rotten mortgages, but they were only the Bad Input. It was the flawed Wall St. System that really was the cause of the Panic. Nonetheless, Subprimes played a critical role, and therefore it is necessary to understand them and why they failed. Subprimes alone would have guaranteed us a Recession. But Subprimes alone would not have caused a Panic.

Definition: Subprime Mortgage

A Subprime Mortgage is one that does not meet the standards of a normal mortgage. The Subprime borrower is, at best, marginally qualified for the loan. The borrower has little or no money for a downpayment and a poor or marginal credit history. FICO [6-1] credit scores of 640 or lower are considered Subprime. While the failure rate of normal mortgages might be 2%, it averaged something like 15% for Subprime mortgages in the late 1990s and early 2000s. The Subprimes of the 2005-2007 time period have a cumulative failure rate of between 50 -100% [6-2].

If Subprime Mortgages always had a high failure rate, why didn't we have the 2008 Panic sooner? The answer is that the Subprime Mortgages were fewer in number. Also, the Subprime Mortgages were not embedded in Derivatives until about 2005. What this book will focus on are the Subprimes primarily issued in 2005 and 2006 [6-3]. This is when more Subprimes of even worse quality (NINJA loans) were issued and then embedded in Derivatives (discussed in Chapter 8 of this book). It was the extremely high failure rates of these Subprimes that led to the failure of Mortgage Derivatives which in turn led to the failure of Wall St. Investment Banks.

Definition: Foreclosure
When a borrower fails to make his mortgage payments, he generally has 3 to 4 months to correct the situation. If he doesn't, the bank can take over the house. Generally, the bank will resell the house ASAP. However, the bank can drag out the foreclosure process.

Definition: Default
When a borrower does not make his monthly mortgage payment for the first time, he is in default. He can correct this situation and not go into foreclosure.

Definition: Failure
This is my definition. This is when a mortgage is either in foreclosure or default. Failure of a mortgage is bad news for a Derivative based on mortgages

---

Definition: NINJA Mortgage
NINJA means NI = No Income, and NJA means No Job or Assets. It is the poorest quality of Subprime Loan, and the most popular in 2005 and 2006 [6-3].

The Role of Congress
The origin of Subprime Mortgages was with Congress. Their objective was to increase the number of Americans that owned their own home. I totally agree with this objective, but I totally disagree with the irresponsible manner in which Congress tried to attain this objective.

Figure 6.1 NINJA Loans

Banks did not want to make Subprime Loans because of the high failure rate. However, Congress essentially forced them to do so with the Community Reinvestment Act and other means. Congress also pressured Fannie and Freddie to buy these Subprime Mortgages on the Secondary Market. Congress did not, however, force Wall St.

Investment Banks to wrap these Subprime Mortgages into Opaque Derivatives.

Definition: Secondary Market
A bank or mortgage company can issue a normal or Subprime Mortgage. If they resell it to Fannie or Freddie or other buyers (like Wall St.), these second buyers are called the Secondary Market.

Description: Fannie Mae and Freddie Mac
Fannie Mae was set up as a government run entity during the Great Depression to encourage home ownership by buying mortgages in the Secondary Market. Freddie Mac was set up in the 1970s for some competition. Then they were transformed into quasi-independent entities until the 2008 Panic when they were again taken over by the government. Between them, Fannie and Freddie hold about half the mortgages in the US or about $5 Trillion of the total $10 Trillion mortgage market. See the Fact Table at the end of the book.

The American Dream – Owning your own home
I remember the day when I bought my first home. After years of living in apartments, I finally had my own home. I was proud. In my decade as a real estate agent, over 90% of my buyers were buying their home for this first time. We celebrated their move-in each time. My wife never lived in a home that she or her family owned until we were married. I know firsthand the joy and pride she felt to be in the first home that was hers.

The Congressionally sponsored Subprime Loans were a large reason why home ownership rose from about 65% to 69%. However, the cost was catastrophic. Americans lost about $14 Trillion in wealth because of the 2008 Panic. An additional 5% of Americans lost their jobs raising the unemployment rate to 10%. In looking at the totality of the situation, was this a good business move? Of course not.

Increasing Home Ownership in a responsible manner

I have an advantage over 90% of our members of Congress. Most of them are professional politicians. They have never run a business and have trouble differentiating between a business and a charity. They don't have 10 years of real estate experience or 14 years of Financial Planning experience. Since Congress seems befuddled about how to increase home ownership in a responsible manner, I have outlined a method in Appendix 1.

Recommendation: Subprime Failure Rate Investigation
An independent commission (e.g., members from accounting firms and not HUD or the Fed or appointed by Congress) should investigate and quantify the failure rate of Subprime loans. At present, the cumulative failure rate of Subprime Mortgages is being kept secret by our government including HUD and the Fed. It is probably greater than a 50% failure rate.

Recommendation: Investigation of Congress
An independent commission (e.g., members from accounting firms) should investigate laws and actions by Congress to determine if undue influence was used to require banks to make Subprime loans and Fannie/Freddie to buy them. Congress should not investigate itself.

Selling Subprimes

Initially banks and mortgage companies were reluctant to sell Subprime Mortgages. That changed when the real estate market just seemed to be on a permanent upward trajectory.

The Southern California Real Estate Market

Southern California was one of the epicenters of the Subprime Meltdown (40% of Subprimes were in California + Florida). I am familiar with this market. My estimate of real estate prices is shown in the graph below. The vertical axis is the price of houses in $ thousands. In 1970, a house cost $100,000. By 1980 it was $200,000. By 1990, it was $400,000. By 2005, it was $800,000. The housing price rises seem to be about 5 years long except for the 1995 to 2005 time period. In each period of prices rising, the housing prices doubled.

House Value
($ thousands)

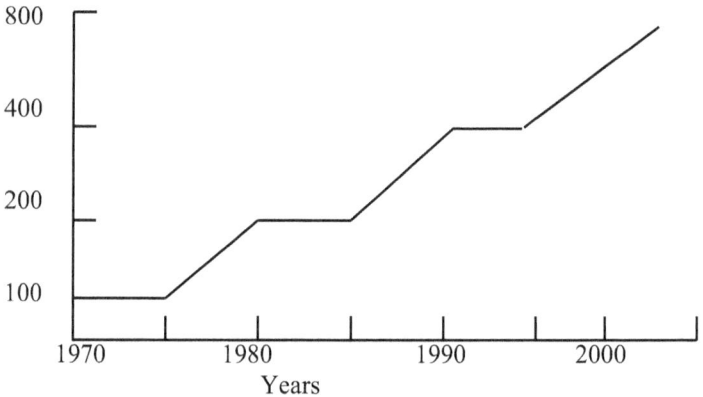

Figure 6.2

What made the 1995-2005 period a 10 year price rise was 9/11. To compensate for the economic carnage of 9/11, the Fed (Greenspan) cut rates very low. The most immediate economic beneficiary of this act was the real estate market. Lower mortgage rates meant that more people could afford to buy a house. More buyers meant the prices kept rising beyond the normal 5 year cycle.

What did this mean for Subprime buyers? If a Subprime buyer bought a house for $200,000 in the year 2000, it was probably up 50% or worth $300,000 by 2005. Talk about the joy of ownership. The word got out, and the number of Subprime buyers multiplied.....just at the wrong time.

Irresponsible Lenders
Here is the opportunity irresponsible lenders saw. More Subprime buyers wanted to buy. Congress wanted them to buy. Congress wanted Fannie and Freddie to buy these loans on the Secondary Market. NINJA loans were OK. Now how hard is it to qualify a Subprime buyer when you don't have to supply any income documentation? How hard is it to qualify a buyer for zero downpayment? If you had a pulse, you got a mortgage.

Irresponsible Lenders put a huge emphasis on Subprime Loans. Even though buyers had to come up with zero downpayment, some buyers still had problems with the monthly mortgage payments. No problem. Lenders came up with teaser rates.

Definition: Teaser Rates and Reset Point
A normal mortgage might have a mortgage rate of 6%. A Subprime borrower might have to pay a higher rate, say 8%. This might be too high for them. No problem. The irresponsible lender would give them a teaser rate of 4% for the first 6 months or maybe 2 years. At the 6 month point (or 2 year point), the mortgage rate would reset to 8% or a variable rate. This point in time is called the reset point.

Since housing prices were climbing at 10% a year, the irresponsible lender and irresponsible real estate agent would tell the Subprime Buyer something like this:

Prices are rising at 10% a year. Your $200,000 house will be $240,000 when your teaser rate resets 2 years from now. Then you can refinance at a lower mortgage rate.

This strategy actually worked in 2005 and 2006, but it fell apart in 2007 when housing prices not only failed to rise but started to fall. The years of 2008 and 2009 were disasters. The housing prices dropped an average of 20% nationwide and more in Subprime areas.

Tossing the Hot Potato
In olden days we had Savings and Loan Associations. These entities would issue mortgages and keep them. The 21st Century approach was different. Generally, the issuer of the Subprime Mortgage would try to toss it to the next buyer (Secondary Market) as soon as possible and make their money on the initial packaging fees. Prominent buyers were Fannie, Freddie and the Wall St. banks that were packaging these mortgages into Derivatives. As it turned out, many of these lenders did not toss fast enough and got caught with an inventory of bad mortgages. Countrywide, New Century, IndyMac Bank and others failed.

Summary
Subprime Loans were and are a disaster. The whole process must be thoroughly investigated and quantified. I've tried diligently to find the failure rate of Subprime Mortgages on www.federalreserve.gov and www.hud.gov and have been unsuccessful. Why it is almost like they are hiding the data. We need to let this data see the light of day (like a Freedom of Information Act for Subprime Failures), and make all Americans aware of it. When this happens, it will be apparent (if it isn't already) that the Subprime process needs complete reform. We need to get America back to its basics. Instead of giving people houses with zero downpayment, they need to "earn it". Please read

Appendix 1 on a sensible plan for increasing home ownership. Please read Appendix 2 which describes how Subprime NINJA borrowers could not lose money. The first reason for the Wall St. Panic was a Bad Input.

Bad Input: Subprime Mortgages

Chapter 7. Cause (1): Leverage

Exec Summary: This chapter will describe the concept of Leverage and the Balance Sheet. This will form the basis for describing the Financial Cause (1) Balance Sheet Abuse or Leverage.

This Chapter has three Sections:

Section 7.1 is a verbal description of *Leverage* and *Balance Sheets*.
Section 7.2 is a more thorough description with numerical examples.

Section 7.3 describes: **Financial Cause (1): Balance Sheet Abuse.**

7.1 Leverage and Balance Sheet

Leverage
In the financial world, leverage means buying an asset without paying completely with your cash. A person who paid 100% cash for a house would be using no leverage at all. Most people can't do this. They usually make a small cash downpayment and borrow money from a bank to pay the remainder of the price. They are using leverage.

Key point
Leverage cuts both ways. This means that Leverage will help the buyer/company when the asset(s) go up in value, but it will hurt when the asset(s) go down in value.

Example: House Purchase with Leverage.
If you buy a house and put $10,000 down, this is your Capital or Net Worth or Equity in the property. If, however, the house drops $10,000 in value, your Capital is wiped out. The same is true for a company. If they operate their company with very little of their own cash, they can be wiped out easily. This is termed excessive leverage.

The bankruptcy of Lehman Brothers which precipitated the whole Panic was due to excessive leverage.

Balance Sheet
The Balance Sheet is the basic tool of all businesses to keep track of their financial status. There are three elements of a Balance Sheet: Assets, Debt (or Liabilities) and Capital (or Net Worth or Equity). Assets and Capital are the good things to have. Debt is a bad thing. For a business, an Asset could be a hotel. A mortgage owed on the hotel would be the Debt. The Capital is the difference between the Asset value and the Debt value or:

Balance Sheet Equation
Assets – Debt = Capital...... or Assets = Debt + Capital

This Balance Sheet Equation is just Guido's Vertical Balance Sheet (i.e., Figure 5.3) written horizontally.

A business usually has several Assets (e.g., hotel, cash) and several Debts (e.g., 1st mortgage, 2nd mortgage). It has, however, only one bottomline number for Capital. Generally, the Balance Sheet for a company is summarized on one page as shown in Figure 7.1 below.

Balance Sheet		
Assets	**Debt**	
x		x
x		x
x	**Capital**	
x		x
Total 123	Total	123

Figure 7.1

Generally, the Assets are shown on the left side and the combination of Debt and Capital on the right side. The numbers on both the left and right sides of the Balance Sheet must equal each other as shown by the number 123 below.

For a business, the value of the Assets must always exceed the value of the Debt or the Capital will be negative. If the Capital is negative, the business is headed for bankruptcy. If a homeowner has negative Capital in his property, however, it does not necessarily mean that he will be foreclosed on. As long as he makes the payments, he keeps the property.

Lehman Brothers ran its business in an extremely risky and irresponsible manner with Capital of only 2%. This meant that the amount of Capital was only 2% of the value of the Assets. Thus, if its real estate Assets dropped only 2% in value, it was headed for bankruptcy which is where it ended up.

7.2   Leverage and Balance Sheet Examples

This section will illustrate leverage for 3 Cases of home ownership. Case 1 will be the initial purchase. Case 2 will show how the Balance Sheet changes when the house *goes up in value*. Case 3 will demonstrate the painful changes on the Balance Sheet when the house *goes down in value*.

Leverage and your mortgage (Case 1)
Nearly every American who owns a house also has a mortgage. Essentially, this is using Leverage to buy your house. Let's illustrate this with an example. Let's say I buy a $200,000 house in 1995 with a 10% downpayment or $20,000 (my Capital). I get an 80% 1st mortgage for $160,000 and a 10% 2nd mortgage for $20,000. I give the

48

seller $20,000 of my own money (a 10% downpayment) and $180,000 of the bank's money ($160,000 mortgage + $20,000 mortgage). This is shown below in two formats:

Balance Sheet in 1995 – Case 1		
Assets	**Debt**	
House $200,000	1st mortgage	$160,000
	2nd mortgage	$ 20,000
	Capital	
		$ 20,000
Total $200,000	Total	$200,000

Figure 7.2

Guido's Vertical Balance Sheet – Case 1		
Assets		
House		$200,000
- Debt		
1st Mortgage	$160,000	
2nd Mortgage	$20,000	
Subtotal Debt	$180,000.........	$180,000
Capital		$ 20,000

Figure 7.3

Figure 7.2 is the conventional Balance Sheet format. Figure 7.3 is Guido's Vertical Balance Sheet. These are two different ways of saying the same thing.

Leverage can help (Case 2)

Let's say I bought my $200,000 house in California in 1995. By January 2007, the average house price had gone up roughly 100%. This would mean that my $200,000 house (1995) was now worth *$400,000* (2007). In investment terms, I turned my $20,000 of equity into *$220,000* of equity. This is shown in Figure 7.4 below.

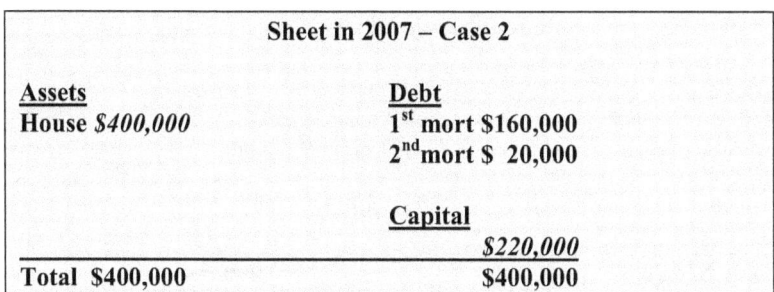

Figure 7.4

A comparison of Figure 7.2 and 7.4 shows I gained 10 times my original investment. Does this really happen? Yes, I've done it twice. This gain is shown in the Balance Sheet of Figure 7.4 with changes in italics.

Leverage can hurt (Case 3)

Let's say I was a little less fortunate in the timing of my house purchase. I bought a $200,000 house in January 2007 with the same financing or debt. In January of 2009, my house had dropped in value by 20%. It is worth only *$160,000*. My Capital in the house is a *minus $20,000 or ($20,000)*. If I had to sell, I would either have to pay $20,000 to the 2nd mortgage holder or be foreclosed on (unless the bank was willing to do a short sell and eat the loss). This is shown in Figure 7.5 below. The purpose of this example is to show that Leverage can hurt as well as help. *__Leverage cuts both ways__*. Does this happen? It is happening all over America right now. It happened to me (my loss was 15% in 1982, but I didn't have to sell).

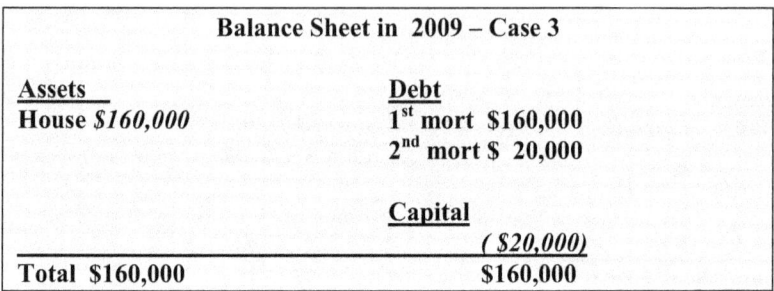

Figure 7.5

Guido's First Balance Sheet for Figures 7.2, 7.4, 7.5

If the Balance Sheets for Cases 1,2,3 above seem a bit confusing, let's just go back to the format of Guido's Vertical Balance Sheet which was the Subtraction Equation. Instead of writing out the numbers in hundreds of thousands, I have simplified a bit (e.g., $200,000 becomes 200). The three cases are shown below:

Guido's Vertical Balance Sheet for Cases 1,2,3			
	Case 1	Case 2	Case 3
Assets	200	400	160
- Debt	180	180	180
Capital	20	220	- 20 or (20)

Figure 7.6

Please note that the Debt is constant at 180 for all three cases above. Then note that when the Asset changes value in the top row, it causes the Capital to change in the bottom row. That's what is important to understand. It is a little easier with Guido's First Balance Sheet to see this than with normal Balance Sheets, but remember that the accountants have to earn a living.

Balance Sheet Characteristics

Note that my negative Capital is -$20,000, but it is shown on the Balance Sheet as a number in ($20,000) in Figures 7.5 and 7.6. This is the standard way of expressing a negative number in accounting. There are some aspects of Balance Sheets that should be noted. First, a Balance Sheet is simply a snapshot at a specific point in time. As time and Asset values change, the Balance Sheet does also. Second, it is important to focus on the Capital value on the Balance Sheet, especially for a bank. If the Capital turns negative, the bank is headed for bankruptcy. Third, if Asset values drop on a Balance Sheet, they will cause an equal drop in the value of the Capital. A smart bank will have enough Capital to cushion a drop in Asset values and a dumb bank won't. In Section 7.3, we will talk about two dumb investment banks – Bear Stearns and Lehman Brothers.

7.3 Financial Cause (1) Balance Sheet Abuse

The thesis of this book is that a Bad Input (Subprimes) was amplified by a poor Wall St. financial System. There are three Financial Causes why this system is poor. Financial Cause (1) is Leverage or Balance Sheet Abuse. Now every reader should know what a Balance Sheet is and what its most critical parameter is – the value of the Capital.

Balance Sheet for Bear Stearns

Do I know exactly what the Balance Sheet for Bear Stearns looked like as it headed for failure in March of 2008? No. See Wikipedia: "Bear Stearns" for one estimate of capital and leverage in Dec 2007. We do know that Bear had insufficient Capital to cover the loss in value of their Assets which included Subprime Loans. We also know that JP Morgan was willing to take over Bear Stearns if the Fed lent it $30 Billion. We also know that Bear operated as an Investment Bank with approximately 2% Capital, a ridiculously thin margin of safety. Also, Bear Stearns had approximately $400 Billion in assets at the time of its demise. Additionally, Bear relied extensively on Overnight or short term Repo financing which might have been in the neighborhood of $40 Billion. With these numbers and some Ball Park Thinking, it is possible to make an informed estimate of what Bear's Balance Sheet might have looked like. This estimate is shown below in Figure 7.7.

**Estimate of Bear Stearn's Balance Sheet in March 2008
(in $Billions)**

Assets	Debt	
$400	Long Term	$350
	Overnight	$ 40
	Capital	
		$ 10
Total $400		$400

Figure 7.7

Now this estimate of Bear's Balance Sheet is very simplified and approximate, but I think it is enough in the Ball Park to illustrate a number of issues. First, Bear's leverage was extremely high at 40 to 1 (Assets/Capital = 400/10). Or stated another way, just a little more than a 2% (or 0.02) drop in asset value would wipe out Bear's Capital entirely (i.e., 0.025 x $400 = $10). Bear was heavily invested in real estate including Subprime Mortgages. As I discussed in the Subprime Chapter, the failure rate for conventional mortgages was about 2% whereas the Subprime failure rate might be as high as 50%. What this meant is that the value of the $400 Billion of Bear's Assets was dropping, and it didn't have to drop much (e.g., 2%) because Bear had almost no Capital to absorb losses.

This is the first part of what I describe as Balance Sheet Abuse or Excessive Leverage. Bear's Capital of only 2% was totally inadequate to absorb a downturn in the market. Normal banks had at least a Capital value (i.e., Capitalization) of 8% of Assets. In Bear's case, this would mean a Capital of $32 Billion.

Definition: Capitalization
The ratio of Capital to Assets is known as Capitalization. From the Bear Balance Sheet, Capital/Assets = 10 /400 = 0.025 or approximately 2%.

Overnight Lending and Bear
The second part of Bear's Balance Sheet Abuse was its excessive dependence on Overnight Lending. What does Overnight Lending mean? It means just what it says. The loan is only good for one day. The next day, Bear must return to the lender and get a new one day loan. On Bear's Balance Sheet, I show Overnight Lending of $40 Billion or 10% of the value of Bear's Assets.

Defintion: Overnight Lending
A loan that is only good for one day.

Can you imagine financing your home mortgages that way? Please go back in this Chapter and look at Figure 7.2 **Balance Sheet in 1995 – Case 1**. Note that the 2nd Mortgage is $20,000 or 10% of the value of the house asset. What would your neighbors say if you told them that you had to refinance your 2nd mortgage every single day? They would probably say that you were nuts. Let me say that I think Bear Stearns was nuts. Their reliance on

Overnight Lending was Financial Russian Roulette. If, on any given day, their Overnight Lenders decided not to lend to them, they were out of business. That's exactly what happened. As Bear's Asset values dropped, the Overnight Lenders decided they did not want their money to go down with the Bear Stearns' ship when it sank. They put their hands in their pockets, and Bear sank.

Definition: Balance Sheet Abuse
In general, this means running a bank in an irresponsible manner with inadequate Capital. Specifically, it means the following:

(1) No bank should be run with only 2% Capital. The minimum Capital should be 8% of Assets.
(2) No bank should rely on Overnight Lending except for some amount that amounts to less than 1% of Asset value. Bear and Lehman were using Overnight Lending that was approximately 10% of their Asset value. This is financial madness.

If it was stupid for Bear Stearns to run their investment bank with only 2% Capital, was it also illegal? The answer is No. Why? Well, in 2004, the Securities and Exchange Commission (SEC) lowered the Capital requirement to about 2% Capital for investment banks (Bear, Lehman, Morgan Stanley, Merrill Lynch and Goldman Sachs). Was this a wise decision? No, it was idiotic. Every taxpayer is paying for this SEC mistake!

The SEC and Haystacks
Here is an idea of the incompetence of the SEC during the 2000-2008 time period. They lowered the required Capital of Investment Banks to 2%. They completely missed the $50 Billion Ponzi scheme of Madoff while nailing Martha Stewart. They did away with the uptick rule [7-1] for short

sales. It's not like the SEC can't find a needle in the haystack. They can't even find the haystack. The new SEC chief, Mary Schapiro, is doing better [7-2].

Balance Sheet for Lehman Brothers
An estimate for the Lehman Brothers Balance Sheet is given below.

Estimate of Lehman's Balance Sheet (Sept 08) (in Billions)		
Assets	**Debt**	
Real Estate $560	Long Term $569	
Derivatives $100	Overnight $ 75	
	Equity	
		$ 16
Total $660	$ 660	

Figure 7.8

I want to make a few observations:

(1) Lehman was leveraged at least 41 to 1 (660/16 = 41)
(2) Lehman had $75 Billion in overnight lending
(3) Lehman said its assets were worth $660 Billion

Was Lehman guilty of Balance Sheet Abuse as I have defined it? Yes, its Capital was barely above 2%. It borrowed even more than 10% of its asset value via Overnight Lending.

A Recession vs. a Panic
There's a big difference between a Recession and a Panic. Recessions generally happen over a period of time. The definition is two quarters of negative GDP growth or at least a 6 month period of time. The Panic of September of

2008 happened in one week. That's quite a difference. A Recession is no fun to get through, but we do it all the time. But the average Recession doesn't drop the stock market by 50%. The average Recession doesn't cause a $700 Billion TARP bailout or an $800 Billion Stimulus/Pork Bill. Therefore it is important to understand the reasons why we had a Panic instead of a Recession. If I was limited to explaining the cause of the Panic for one single reason, it would be:

Balance Sheet Abuse

Lehman failed **_suddenly_** because its Overnight Lending stopped **_suddenly_**. If it had an 8% Capital cushion and no Overnight Lending, it might have survived.

It's over one year later and absolutely nothing has been done to change the rules. Who could influence this change? Here's a partial list: Accounting Boards, the Financial Media, Congress and the SEC.

Let me just address the Accounting Boards first (US and International). Why has nothing been said about 2% capitalization? Why has absolutely nothing been said about the insane reliance on Overnight Lending? These Boards don't need Congress to act. They can take their own steps. Why haven't they??? It would be better if they acted rather than Congress. My grade on their effort is F.

Where has the Financial Media been on this issue? Are they just reporters regurgitating what they have been told or can anyone out there do some independent thinking and analysis. Our Financial Media should be our watchdog. It should be our first line of defense against abuse and stupidity. My grade on their effort is F.

Congress gets an F. Based on its past performance, the SEC gets an F-, but I hope Mary Schapiro can improve this agency.

TARP saved Wall St. from Balance Sheet Abuse

TARP did half the job, but it did no rule changes. It flooded the system with nearly $1 Trillion in liquidity for capitalization. However, the TARP solution is analogous to pumping up a punctured tire without first fixing the puncture. As long as you can pump real fast (i.e., flood the system with liquidity), you don't have to fix the puncture (Balance Sheet Abuse). It is a solution, but it is a dumb way to do business.

My definition of Balance Sheet Abuse was twofold:
(1) 2% equity
(2) Overnight Lending

As a practical matter, the 2% equity problem has been solved for the 5 Investment Banks because they are no longer Investment Banks. Bear and Lehman failed (the remnants of Bear were scooped up by JP Morgan). Merrill Lynch was smart enough to merge with Bank of America. Morgan Stanley and Goldman Sachs converted themselves into conventional banks which are required to have 8% equity. *__However, we still need the rule change to outlaw any bank ever using just 2% equity again (unless we want another Panic).__*

The Overnight Lending issue has not been solved by TARP at all.

Summary

This chapter first addressed the concepts of Leverage and Balance Sheet. These concepts are a necessary first step to understand the Balance Sheet Abuse that was at the heart of the Wall St. Panic. The first of the three most important causes of our present flawed financial system on Wall St is:

Financial Cause (1) Balance Sheet Abuse or Leverage
   (a) only 2% capitalization by banks
   (b) relying on Overnight Lending for 10% of debt

The rule changes necessary to correct Balance Sheet Abuse have not been taken. If we don't want another Panic, someone has to wake up and take some action. The Fed flooding our banking system with liquidity is a temporary solution to a permanent problem. The Dodd Bill in Congress does not address this issue at all!

Chapter 8. Cause (2) Derivatives

Exec Summary: This Chapter will discuss Derivatives, Securitization and why Mortgage Derivatives were opaque.

There are two sections in this Chapter:

8.1 will focus on the general concept of Derivatives with a REIT as an example of a simple, plain vanilla Mortgage Derivative.
8.2 will describe some of the complexities of the Opaque Mortgage Backed Derivatives that were at the root of the 2008 Panic.

8.1 Derivatives
What are Derivatives? Why did they break our financial system. This section will address the first question.

What are Derivatives? Few Americans know. In 2008, I was on a tour of Greece with 25 other Americans. It was a very interesting and varied group of people. One was even from the SEC. In fact, he was one of the top 6 managers there. I eagerly asked him to explain to me what a Derivative was. He couldn't [3]. This certainly says a lot about the SEC, but it is also an indication of the almost complete ignorance of what Derivatives are by the general public. The makers of these Derivatives will continue to cause financial mayhem until you the Public understand them better and insist on regulation. Not all Derivatives are bad as will be illustrated by the REITs and Futures discussed in this section.

Simplified Definition of Derivatives
It is a contract based on an asset, index or condition.

---

[3] In fairness, his specialty was Human Resources.

> **Example 1. Mortgage Backed Derivative**
> If I have a pool of mortgages, I can form a Derivative based on the value of these mortgages (asset).

> **Example 2. Futures Contract on Oil Prices**
> If I am an airline, I can hedge against the price of oil going up by buying a Futures Contract on the price of oil at $80 per barrel (condition). If the price of oil goes up beyond $80 per barrel, the seller of the contract pays me the difference.

Not all Derivatives are bad or unregulated

Example 2 is a regulated Derivative known as a Futures Contract. The Commodities Futures Trading Commission (CFTC) is the regulator and does a good job (see Appendix 3. CFTC Regulation). Futures Contracts have been around from the 1850s and work. They are easily understood, regulated and their price is known since they are publicly traded on an exchange. The Opaque Mortgage Backed Derivatives are just the opposite. They are hard to understand, not regulated and no one knows their price since they are traded secretly between two parties (i.e., Dark Pool Trading).

Why weren't Mortgaged Backed Derivatives regulated?

There was an attempt to do just this, and it failed. Brooksley Born, head of the CFTC in the late 1990s, tried to do just this. Her effort was quashed by Secretary of the Treasury Rubin (former head of Goldman Sachs), Fed Chairman Alan Greenspan and Larry Summers (current head of the Council of Economic Advisors). But don't take my word for it. Go and buy the DVD from PBS that tells the whole story (www.pbs.org, go to "shop", search for "The Warning"). Talk about a fork in the road. If Mortgage Backed Derivatives had been regulated in the

1990s, we probably wouldn't have had the Panic and 10% unemployment.

Scope of Derivative Discussion in this Chapter

There are a mind boggling $600 Trillion of Derivatives in our financial system. The Panic was caused primarily by just $2 Trillion of Opaque Subprime Mortgage Derivatives. Does this mean that we don't have to worry about the other $598 Trillion of Derivatives? Absolutely not. Chapter 9 will discuss some of the $30 Trillion of CDS Derivatives that also contributed to the Panic, but this Chapter will be limited to just Mortgage Backed Derivatives.

Derivative Concept and a Car Lease

The essence of a Derivative is that it is "derived" from something that you do not own. Let me illustrate this by comparing a Car Lease to a Bond.

Definition: Bond

A bond is a debt instrument of a certain value (e.g., $1,000) that pays a guaranteed rate of interest (e.g., 5% per year) for a fixed amount of time (e.g., 3 years), and the investor receives back his principal ($1,000) when the bond matures (reaches the end of the 3 year period).

Comparing a Car Lease to a Bond Derivative

When you lease a car, you don't own it, but you get the benefit of owning it. You get to drive it. Of course to lease it, you have to pay a lease fee. Also, when it comes time to turn the car back in, you have to pay the depreciation and pay for any damage.

Now let's say you want to lease a Bond. In other words, you want to get the benefit from a Bond (i.e., the 5% interest), but you don't want to own it. You pay a lease fee (e.g., 1% of the Bond value), and you are on the hook for any loss in value of the Bond when your contract ends.

On the face of it, whether you lease a car or a bond seems pretty similar. Here's one important difference. Let's say you have an accident with your leased car which is totaled. You're stuck for the $500 deductible, but your insurance company pays for the rest of the car. Now if a Bond fails (e.g., say it was based on a Subprime Mortgage), you're stuck for the entire loss. That's a lot different, and, in essence, it is a prime reason why Bear and Lehman failed.

Hopefully, the concept of "Derivative" is becoming a little clearer. A Derivative is not a real financial instrument such as a Bond or a Mortgage. It is based on a Bond or a Mortgage. It is "derived" from the Bond or Mortgage.

Securitization
One of the key reasons given for creating Mortgage Backed Derivatives is Securitization. Securities are either stocks or bonds which can be traded in a minute vs. a Mortgage which might take weeks to trade.

Definition: Securitization
Mortgages are generally big (e.g., $100,000 or more) and are long term (e.g., 30 years). This inhibits many people from buying them as an investment. If a $100,000 Mortgage could be turned into 100 Bonds of $1,000 each, they would be easier to sell. Instead of trying to find one buyer with $100,000 in his pocket, you could search for 100 people with $1,000 in their pockets.

REIT's – a plain vanilla Derivative
Figure 8-1 below is a simplified representation of the Securitization and Derivative process utilized by Real Estate Investment Trusts (REITs). It is sort of like slicing

bread. A Mortgage (the loaf) of $100,000 is sliced into 100 Bonds of $1,000 each (the bread slices). The hard to trade Mortgage is securitized into more easily traded Bonds. The Bonds are "derived" from the Mortgage so they can be thought of as a plain vanilla Mortgage Derivative. The owner of an REIT share (or Mortgage Derivative) doesn't really own a mortgage. He owns a Derivative based on a portion of that Mortgage.

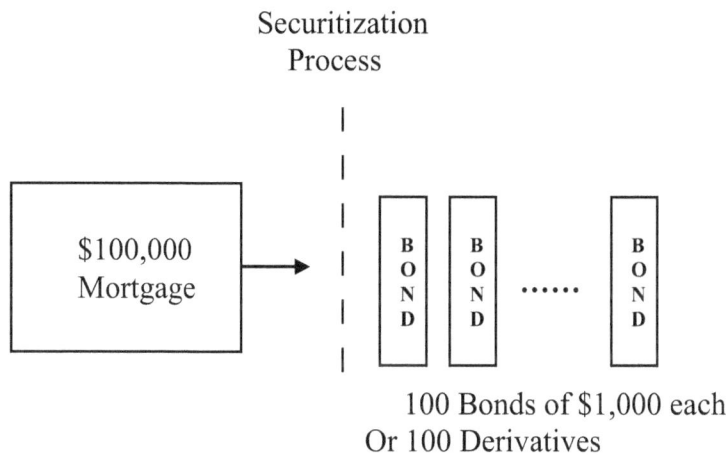

Securitization
Process

100 Bonds of $1,000 each
Or 100 Derivatives

Figure 8.1 REIT Slices

Of course, real world REITs are based on a pool of mortgages not simply one mortgage as shown in Figure 8.1. The mortgages in the pool are generally of the same quality (e.g., AA rating) so the buyers of the REIT Bonds (or shares or Derivatives) understands what he is getting.

Differences: REIT vs. Opaque Mortgage Derivatives
I have used a REIT to illustrate a plain vanilla Mortgage Backed Derivative. There are some important differences between it and the Opaque Mortgage Backed Derivatives discussed in the next section. First, REITs are easy to understand and easy to rate for quality. Second, REITs are

regulated. Third, REITs are traded on public exchanges so their prices are known to all. Opaque Mortgage Backed Derivatives are hard to understand, hard to rate for quality, unregulated and difficult to value since they are only traded secretly between two parties.

8.2 Opaque Mortgage Backed Derivatives

Opaque Mortgage Backed Derivatives are more complex than the plain vanilla REIT described above. Like the REIT, Mortgage Backed Derivatives start with a pool of mortgages. However, what is different is the slicing technique.

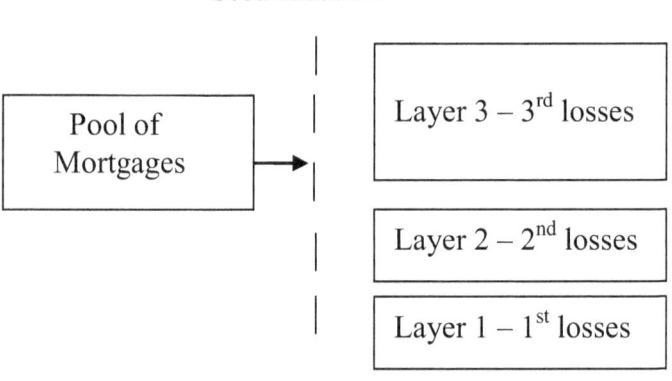

Figure 8.2 Derivative Slices

These layer slices are not like the straight forward bread slices of REITs. One slice of REIT bread was 1/100 of the Mortgage Pool. One layer of the Mortgage Backed Derivative is fundamentally different. Layer 1 receives the first 10% of the losses from the entire Mortgage Pool. ___**In other words, if the pool contains 1,000 Mortgages and there are 10% losses, Layer 1 receives all of those losses. It is wiped out.**___ The next 10% of all losses goes to Layer 2. Layer 3 is unaffected unless the losses exceed 20% of the value of the pool. To illustrate the difference between

REIT slices and Derivative slices, both are shown below for the case when 15% of the Mortgage Pool has failed with the shading representing the 15% losses.

Securitization

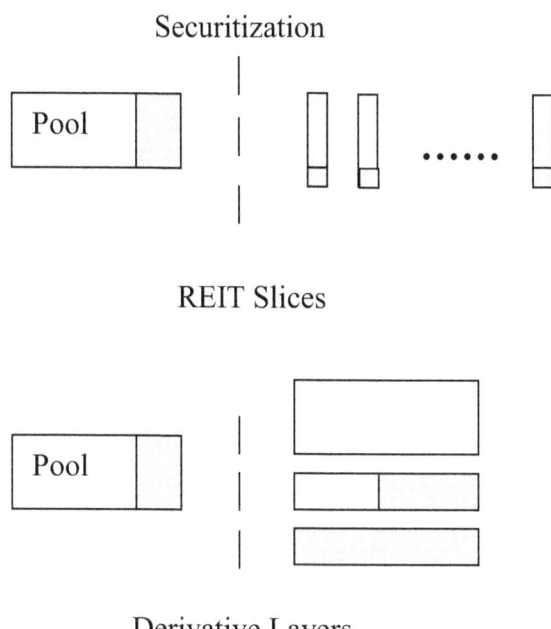

REIT Slices

Derivative Layers

Figure 8.3 Comparing REIT & Derivative Slices

To understand why Mortgage Backed Derivatives were so treacherous, it is essential to understand Figure 8.3. As shown, if there are 15% losses in the Pool, each REIT slice gets a 15% loss as denoted with the shaded area. However, in the Derivative Layers, the losses are shared quite differently. ***Since Layer 1 receives the first 10% of all losses, it is 100% wiped out.*** The next 5% of the losses goes to Layer 2 which is half wiped out. This is why the owner of the wrong Layer of a Mortgage Backed Derivative can easily get 100% wiped out.

Each Layer of a Mortgage Backed Derivative can be sold separately as a Collateral Debt Obligation or CDO. "CDO" is just another term for Mortgage Backed Derivatives.

Concentrated Losses
If a Subprime Mortgage failed, it did not mean that the Mortgage value loss was 100%. Generally the losses ranged from 20 to 50%. However Layers of a Mortgage Backed Derivative could have 100% losses because all the losses flowed to the 1st Layer then the 2nd Layer as shown in Figures 8.2 & 8.3. For example, if a Subprime Mortgage Pool lost 30% in value, at least 3 Layers would be affected.

Goldman Sachs Abacus CDO
Recently, the SEC has brought a case against Goldman Sachs concerning the Abacus CDO (Mortgage Backed Derivative) which it sold to the German Bank IKB. Although the CDO was rated AAA, it lost 99% of its value a few months after IKB purchased it. Why? It was similar to the Layer 1 illustrated above in Figures 8.2 & 8.3.

More Complexity and Opaqueness
In Appendix 4, I describe some additional complexities of the Mortgage Backed Derivatives that contributed to opaqueness. These Derivatives were sliced, diced and mixed together to prevent any intelligent analysis of their value. For example, one Subprime CDO (e.g., Layer 1 of Figure 8.3) could be combined with other normal Mortgage CDOs to make one giant CDO. The result was opaqueness.

Hamburger, Mad Cow Disease and Opaqueness
Let's say that hundreds of cows are chopped up for hamburger and then it is discovered that one cow had Mad Cow Disease. How could you separate just the Mad Cow hamburger (Subprimes) from the rest? The hamburger is opaque.

Figure 8.4 The effect of Opaque Derivatives

The $5 Trillion Toxic Monster
The cartoon in Figure 8.4 shows how Wall St. turned an approximately $200 Billion Subprime Loss into a $5 Trillion Monster. In Appendix 5, I detail how I estimate the true Subprime Loss for Wall St. at $200 Billion. In

short, Wall St. panicked because of opaqueness of the Mortgage Derivatives. The Panic began in September 2008 when Lehman Brothers went bankrupt. Everyone knew that one of the critical reasons for Lehman failing was Subprime Mortgage Derivatives. The fact that Lehman had only 2% capitalization was conveniently overlooked by the financial media. Instead, it concentrated on those deadly Subprime Mortgages. No one was sure how many real estate Derivatives (both normal and Subprime) were infected with Subprimes (Mad Cow Disease). Irrational fear took over and even affected Commercial Real Estate Derivatives (which had nothing to do with Subprimes at all). Opaqueness help cause a Panic that was not justified.

Financial Cause (2)
What is the second financial cause for the Wall St. Panic of 2008? If you guessed, Opaque Mortgage Backed Derivatives, you are right.

Financial Cause (2) Opaque Mortgage Derivatives
The second major cause for the poor Wall St. financial system which amplified the Bad Input from Subprimes is Opaque Mortgage Derivatives. These Derivatives were overly complex, deceptively marketed, unregulated, opaque and poorly modeled. They were not publicly traded so no good market price could be determined.

Summary
My son who was unfamiliar with Mortgages, Bonds and Derivatives said this Chapter was like drinking water from a fire hose. If you were able to understand that Mortgage Derivatives are derived from a Pool of Mortgages, you picked up one of the critical points. If you came away with the impression that Wall St.'s Mortgage Derivatives were far too complex, you picked up another critical point. If

you understood that the opaqueness of the Mortgage Derivatives magnified the existing problem, you understood the central message.

Addendum

This Chapter has been a Magic + 1 level description of Mortgage Derivatives. I strongly recommend reading the following Appendices that provide additional explanation.

Appendix 3. CFTC Regulation
Appendix 4. Derivative Complexity
Appendix 5 Size of Subprimes
Appendix 6. Derivative Math Models
Appendix 7. Turnings Subprimes into AAA
Appendix 9. Rule of 72

Appendix 3 describes why CFTC regulation of Futures Derivatives works. Appendix 4 goes into some of the additional complexities which helped make Mortgage Derivatives opaque. Appendix 5 describes the size of the Subprime Mortgages, and the size of the Subprime Losses that affected Wall St. Appendix 6 describes the poor quality of math modeling used both in Mortgage Derivative construction and in their evaluation by Rating Agencies. Selling the inferior Subprimes as an AAA rated product played an important role in the Panic. Appendix 7 gives an idea of how this was done. Appendix 9 explains why someone might want to buy a risky CDO.

For those interested in finding out more about Derivatives, I recommend the following reading:

Wikipedia: "Derivatives" and "Mortgage Backed Securities"
"Fool's Gold", by Gillian Tett
"All About Derivatives", by Michael Durbin
"Subprime Derivatives", by Goodman, Li, Fabrozzi et. al

Chapter 9. Cause (3): Credit Default Swaps

Exec Summary: This chapter will discuss why CDS is Financial Cause (3) of the Wall St. Panic. CDS is a much worse financial weapon of mass destruction than Mortgage Backed Derivatives because it is derived not for something tangible like a mortgage but merely a promise (or, in the AIG case, thin air).

This chapter on CDS has several Sections:

9.1 is on inadequate Capital.
9.2 is on hiding CDS from the Balance Sheet.
9.3 discusses the actuarial failure.
9.4 is on lack of "insurable risk".

Definition: Credit Default Swaps (CDS)

Credit Default Swaps are essentially insurance against the failure of a financial instrument such as a Derivative or a Bond. CDS could insure against the failure of a company such as Lehman as well. It is 100% unregulated.

Example: CDS pay out if Lehman fails

Let's say that Company G has a CDS contract for $7 Billion from AIG that will pay off in the event Lehman goes bankrupt. When Lehman fails, AIG must pay Company G $7 Billion immediately, not at the end of a 1 year bankruptcy proceeding.

In my opinion, the failure of AIG had more to do with the Panic of 2008 than the failure of Lehman. Can I prove that? No. Most of what AIG did is being kept secret by the Fed. However, enough information is available to sketch out what happened to AIG and how it related to the Panic.

9. 1 AIG and inadequate Capital

AIG was the largest insurance company in the world with $1 Trillion in assets and maybe $80 Billion in capital. It put itself in mortal danger by owning or issuing $2 Trillion in Derivatives (i.e., more than the worth of its assets). Of those $2 Trillion in Derivatives, a mind boggling $390 Billion were CDS [9-1]. That meant that if it was necessary to pay claims on all $390 Billion of CDS, the $80 Billion [9-2] of capital would not come close to doing the job. What happened was that a few days after the collapse of Lehman, the Fed saved AIG with an immediate $85 Billion bailout which was later raised to $180 Billion. This shows how inadequate the Capital of AIG was. What we do know is that the Fed paid out $40 – 60 Billion to a number of banks including Goldman Sachs, Societe [9-3] and others.

AIG didn't own any Subprimes that failed. It managed to create its losses out of thin air.

Financial Cause (3) Credit Default Swaps

Credit Default Swaps played a critical role in the Wall St. Panic of 2008. CDS brought down the world's largest insurance company, AIG, because it had inadequate Capital to cover its CDS insurance promises. AIG's failure could very possibly have brought down several large banks if the government had not taken AIG over.

The idea of insuring against failure is a pretty old idea. One of the critical questions is whether the party issuing the insurance has adequate money to pay the claims. Let me illustrate this with the following story.

> **My Dad's story with an "insured" investment**
> My Dad was a great stock market investor, but he had not
> diversified into real estate. I recommended that he do this.
> I had in mind that he would buy a small condo and rent it
> out. What he did was invest in shares of 3 Land
> Partnerships formed by another Douglas engineer. The
> plan was for each Partnership to subdivide the land it
> bought. I groaned. The land was in the middle of the
> desert and would serve no economic function. My Dad
> said, "Don't worry." If the subdivided land could not be
> sold by the Partnerships, an insurance company (Fly by
> Nite Insurance) would reimburse the partners their original
> purchase prices. It was "insured" and "guaranteed". Of
> course, there were no buyers for the subdivided land, and
> all of the 3 Partnerships failed. Fly by Nite Insurance
> actually did pay off the first failed Partnership, but went
> belly up, and there was no money for the other two
> Partnerships. It was simply a case of insufficient funds just
> like AIG.

Why is it so important to focus on having "adequate
capital" to pay off CDS claims? The reason is that there is
$30 Trillion of CDS out there in our financial system. Is
there $30 Trillion in capital to pay these claims? No way.
Look at the Fact Table at the end of the book. The value of
our total stock market is $10 Trillion. The capital of our
major banks is less than $1 Trillion. Where is this $30
Trillion supposed to come from? Thin air? It's a joke.
CDS is largely a sham [9-4].

9.2 CDS doesn't show up on the Balance Sheet.
Did the Board of Directors of AIG know that the company
had the potential obligation to pay $390 Billion in CDS
claims? It sure would be an interesting question for
Congress or the Financial Crisis Inquiry Commission to ask
them. My guess is that they didn't know because CDS

doesn't show up on anyone's Balance Sheet. If there is no actual loss (and there weren't losses for a number of years), then why put it on the Balance Sheet. Well, here's one reason. The company has the potential of huge losses. Everyone from the Board of Directors to the stockholders should be aware of this possibility rather than get a huge surprise when the losses hit.

Recommendation: Investigate the AIG Balance Sheet
Since AIG is costing the taxpayers about $180 Billion, the Balance Sheet of AIG should be thoroughly investigated. How much risk was AIG exposed to if all its CDS needed to be paid out? Was any of this risk shown on its Balance Sheet? How much of its CDS actually failed and was paid out and how did this alter its Balance Sheet? How much CDS risk remains on the AIG Balance Sheet? How did the accounting firm of AIG treat this issue? This should become public information since the public owns AIG.

There was some discussion in Congress requiring CDS issuers to show at least 10% of the potential loss on their Balance Sheet. I think this is a sound idea. Also, there should be a footnote describing what the complete loss could be. Furthermore, this is an accounting issue. Accounting boards should be insisting on CDS showing up on Balance Sheets. These Balance Sheets are supposed to give an accurate portrayal of a company's financial position and showing AIG's without including the risk of CDS pay outs is a serious omission.

9.3 CDS Actuarial Failure
CDS was treated like Life Insurance in an actuarial sense. The issuers charged low premiums for assuming high risk. This is done with Life Insurance. If someone owns a Life Insurance policy for $100,000, they typically pay 1% of the face value of the Life Insurance (e.g., $1,000/year) or even

less. How do Life Insurance companies determine what price to charge? They have 100 years of data on the death rates of people. That's good actuarial data.

What kind of actuarial data did AIG have on Subprimes, especially NINJA loans? It had next to nothing. It certainly didn't have 100 years of data. What they probably did was assume that a Subprime Mortgage was just like a normal mortgage with a 2% a year failure rate. They were certainly wrong. The cumulative failure rate for the NINJA loans of the 2005/2006 time period is probably above 50%. Let me give a numerical example.

Example: AIG issues $ 1 Billion of CDS coverage
AIG issues $1 Billion of CDS coverage of Subprime CDOs that incur a 50% failure rate within 3 years. AIG charges only 1% or $10 Million and loses $500 Million. This is a gross actuarial failure.

Again, AIG's mistake was that it insured something that it did not have actuarial data on. There wasn't 100 years of failure rate data on Subprimes, especially NINJA loans. These were relatively new financial products that had existed only a year or two in the case of NINJA loans. In fact, this is probably a basic problem with nearly all CDS issued. They are issuing coverage on new financial products that they don't have adequate actuarial data on. See Appendix 6 for a discussion of Derivative Math Models which also applies to CDS Math Models.

9.4 "Insurable Interest" and CDS
CDS purports to be insurance. It isn't. The prime function of insurance is to compensate for a loss (not provide a profit). One of the core principals of insurance is "insurable interest".

Definition: "Insurable Interest"
A prime requirement for an insurance contract is that the purchaser have an "insurable interest". This means the purchaser owns the item being insured.

Example: My Home Insurance [9-5]
I have insurance on the home I own. My ownership of the house is an "insurable interest". When the Witch Creek Fire of 2007 burned down 6 homes in the next block, I was happy I had insurance. My 6 neighbors did get compensated for their losses and have rebuilt their homes. I could not own insurance on their homes because I did not have an "insurable interest".

Recently, the SEC brought a case against Goldman Sachs regarding the Abacus CDO [9-6]. The case involves misrepresentation by Goldman to its client, but the really important aspect of the case is that it brought the flaw of CDS with regard to "insurable interest" to light.

The Goldman Abacus Case and "Insurable Interest"
Goldman/Paulson/ACA formulated a list of Subprime Derivatives worth $1 Billion that were sold to two banks. There was also $1 Billion of CDS insurance issued, but it was not sold to the banks but rather the Paulson Hedge Fund which had no "insurable interest". When the Subprime Derivatives lost 99% of their value a few months later, one bank failed and the other was seriously damaged. On the other hand, Paulson's Hedge Fund made $1 Billion on the CDS insurance pay out.

This is only one case where Paulson made a killing in CDS. In fact, he made something like $20 Billion for his Hedge Fund using CDS insurance while having absolutely no "insurable interest'. If you don't believe me, please read

"The Greatest Trade Ever" by G. Zuckerman and "The Big Short" by M. Lewis. Now did Mr. Paulson do anything illegal? Well, it is tough to do anything illegal if there are no rules and no regulation [9-7]. However, if anyone thinks this is a good example of why we should support laissez faire, I think they should have their head examined. Having the CDS insurance pay out go to the party with no "insurable interest" is just turning insurance into gambling. Wall St. shouldn't be lionizing Paulson. Las Vegas should.

Recommendation: Investigate CDS Gambling
Congress should investigate how CDS insurance has been turned into a tool of gambling. Specifically, it should correlate CDS pay outs to the owners of the underlying Derivatives that failed or to parties with no "insurable interest". Congress should decide whether the CFTC should regulate CDS or if it should be turned over to the Nevada State Gambling Commission.

Comment: Lipstick on a Snake
Describing CDS as insurance and as adding to the safety of the marketplace isn't putting lipstick on a Pig. It is putting lipstick on a Snake.

Summary
I identify CDS as Financial Cause (3) of the Wall St. Panic.

Financial Cause (3) Credit Default Swaps

In the case of AIG, the company could not honor the insurance promises it made. We know that the Fed used at least $40 - 60 Billion of taxpayer money to honor the CDS contracts that AIG issued without the money to pay them off, but since the government has bailed out AIG to the

Figure 9.1

tune of $180 Billion, the final story could be much worse. What happened to AIG could easily happen again because we have no idea what CDS contracts have insured or how much money the companies that have issued them have available to pay them off in the event of default or downgrade. There is a mind boggling $30 Trillion of CDS in our financial system. Refer to the Fact Table at the end of this book. The $30 Trillion of CDS is more than double our GDP of $14 Trillion and dwarfs the capital of Wall St. Banks (less than $1 Trillion). It dwarfs the recently formed $1 Trillion EU fund to back up the Euro. The ability to pay off $30 Trillion of CDS is just not credible. CDS is a financial weapon of mass destruction waiting to explode again.

Also, as discussed in this Chapter, CDS is also flawed because no "insurable interest" is required, no visibility on Balance Sheets is required and insufficient actuarial data exists on what is being insured. CDS is so flawed that it should be recalled like a bad car made by Detroit.

Recommendation: Ban CDS and start over again

CDS in its present form is so flawed that it should be recalled like a bad car from Detroit. All issuers of CDS should simply refund the premiums they have received and terminate the product. If a new financial insurance product is desired, the financial market needs to start all over again and use the criteria in this Chapter to build a true, credible insurance product regulated by the CFTC (see Appendix 3). The concept of insurance is not flawed. CDS is.

Addendum – CDS and Synthetic Derivatives

Generally, the idea of a CDS is to pay off upon the failure of an underlying security such as a CDO. To get this pay off, the CDS purchaser usually makes an insurance payment. With a Synthetic CDO, this is altered a bit. First, we must start with a real CDO based on a pool of underlying mortgages. Let's just take one layer or tranche of that CDO. Let's say the CDO is worth $1 million and pays 5% interest per year or $50,000 a year. Now we are going to make a Synthetic CDO from this real CDO. We need two parties to bet against each other. Party #1 will pay Party #2 $50,000/year. This $50,000 is like an insurance premium. Party #2 will have to pay Party #1 $1,000,000 if the real CDO fails (like an insurance pay out).

Let's note a few of the Synthetic CDO characteristics. There is no real CDO involved, and therefore no real pool of mortgages. You might think of the Synthetic CDO as a reflection of a real CDO. Second, while a real CDO might claim to be performing "securitization" of mortgages, the Synthetic CDO can make no such claim. It is purely a bet between two parties. In Las Vegas, they call that gambling. On Wall St., it is still gambling, but it is called risk management.

Example. Synthetic Fire Insurance
Let's say I pay $1,000/year for fire insurance on my house, and the insurance company will pay me $500,000 in the event it burns down. Now let's say some Wall St. firm wants to create a synthetic fire insurance CDO based on my fire insurance. They find a Party A that is willing to pay $1,000/year replicating my premium. They also find a Party B that is willing to pay Party A $500,000, replicating my insurance company, if my house burns down. The Wall St. firm sells one end of the Synthetic Fire Insurance CDO to Party A and the other end to Party B and pockets a nice commission.....for adding no value at all. The Synthetic Fire Insurance has no relationship to the real world of insurance. It is just a bet masquerading as finance.

Chapter 10. Analysis of the Wall St. Panic

Exec Summary: **This Chapter will analyze how the Bad Input (Subprimes) and 3 Financial Causes contributed to the Wall St. Panic.**

Scope of Analysis

This Chapter is going to take the four elements of my thesis for the Wall St. Panic and put them together. Again, this is intended to be a Magic +1 level discussion of the Panic. There are many other issues affecting the Panic that are not going to be discussed including: the Housing Asset Bubble, Fannie/Freddie, Too Big to Fail, Off Balance Sheet Accounting, Short Selling, Rating Agencies, the Repo Market, Rehypothecation and more.

The Critical Split of Subprime Losses

In my Fact Table of Financial Elements, I state the size of the Subprime Mortgages at $2 Trillion, and the size of the Subprime losses at 20% or $400 Billion or $0.4 Trillion. The origin of these numbers is discussed further in Appendix 5. What was absolutely critical was the split between the losses that went to Fannie/Freddie and the losses that went to Wall St. I assume that the Subprime losses were split 50/50.

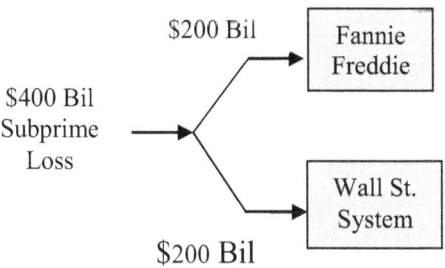

Figure 10.1

While Wall St. would like to project that it suffered the brunt of nearly all the Subprime Losses, this is just not true. Fannie/Freddie were dumb enough to buy half the Subprimes or perhaps even more. However, what is truly important is the different effect these similar size losses had on our financial system.

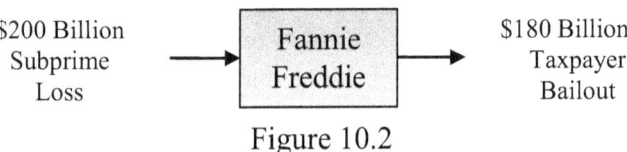

Figure 10.2

As Figure 10.2 shows, the $200 Billion of Subprime Losses input to Fannie/Freddie came out as a $180 Billion loss that resulted in a $180 Billion Taxpayer Bailout. That's bad, but it not nearly the damage we suffered from Wall St.

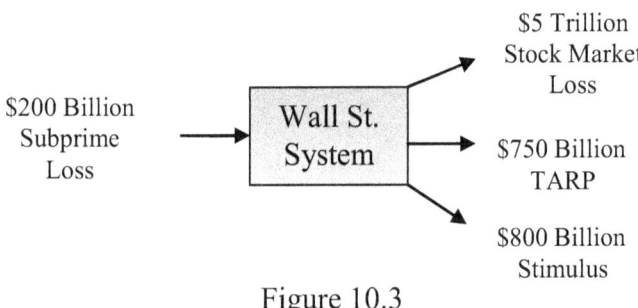

Figure 10.3

Which $200 Billion Subprime Loss had the worst effect? Obviously the answer is the loss that went through the Wall St. System. Fannie/Freddie caused the taxpayers $180 Billion in grief, but Wall St. cost them $6.5 Trillion. The question is why? The answer is that Fannie/Freddie did not cause a Panic, but Wall St. did.

Why did Wall St. cause a Panic?
People panic from fear of the unknown. People knew what the Fannie/Freddie losses were, but they didn't know the

size of the Wall St. losses. There was talk in the press of $5 Trillion in toxic mortgages. This was crazy, but it wasn't contradicted by anyone – the financial media, the Fed or Wall St.

Figure 10.4

What people did see was a Bear Stearns failure followed by a Lehman failure followed by the failure of AIG, the world's largest insurance company. What was going on?

No one had an answer. Well, this book supplies answers at a Magic +1 level.

Why did Bear and Lehman fail?
The readers of this book should know the answer, Financial Cause (1): Balance Sheet Abuse. Bear and Lehman were leveraged to the hilt. Furthermore, they had a huge amount of Overnight Loans. When the Subprime Losses started to hit, they had no capital cushion to absorb them. Their measly 2% capitalization meant their assets had to fall only 2%, and they were out of business. While Subprimes were not their only assets, when these Subprimes fell in value, it was fatal. A more complete description is given in Appendix 8 which compares Bank Capital vs. Subprime Losses.

Why did AIG fail?
The readers of this book should know the answer, Financial Cause (3): Credit Default Swaps (CDS). Stupidly, AIG had made $ Billions in CDS insurance promises that it couldn't keep. A few days after Lehman's failure, the Fed had to rescue AIG to the tune of $85 Billion which was later increased to $180 Billion. Why that is the size of the Fannie/Freddie loss, and AIG didn't even own any Subprime Mortgages. What AIG managed to do is generate losses out of thin air. If Winston Churchill were still around, he probably would have said: Never have so few, lost so much, for so many [10-1].

Why did the stock market Panic and lose 50% in value?
No one knew what was going on. Fear of the unknown causes Panic. Financial Cause (2) Opaque Mortgage Derivatives was a major factor. Because of this opaqueness, the financial media could write about $5 Trillion in toxic mortgages. If the loss size had been known (more like $200 Billion), it would not have caused a

Panic. The loss size at Fannie/Freddie was known vs. the unknown loss of Wall St. Subprime Derivatives. They were sliced and diced into Derivatives so many ways that no one knew their size or their potential loss (closer to $200 Billion than $5 Trillion). Unnecessary complexity and deliberate opaqueness prevented a sensible analysis.

The Bad Input (Subprimes) and other Bad Inputs

The Bad Input for the Panic. was, of course, the Subprime Mortgages. This was the worst mortgage program in the history of the world. However, I do not treat it as one of the Financial Causes of the Wall St. System. Why? Subprimes were only an Input. Something else could also be an Input to the Wall St. System and cause another Panic. See a brief discussion of these in Appendix 10. "Black Swans and Bad Inputs".

Summary

The Wall St. System was and is flawed due to three Financial Causes. The Bad Input, Subprimes, caused the system to Panic.

Wall St. System Flaws

Financial Cause (1) Balance Sheet Abuse
    (a) Only 2% capitalization of investment banks
    (b) Overnight lending accounted for over 10% of
    the debt for Bear and Lehman (and maybe others)

Financial Cause (2) Opaque Mortgage Backed Derivatives

Financial Cause (3) Credit Default Swaps

Bad Input: Subprime Mortgages

Figure 10.5

The above cartoon captures the situation as described by this book. The Fed is madly pumping taxpayer money into the Wall St. System (tire) without first fixing the three Financial Causes (punctures).

Part 3. Why Wall St. will Panic again

The primary reason why Wall St. will Panic again is that none of the prime causes for the 2008 Panic have been fixed. This Part begins with a discussion of what the Fed did and didn't do in response to the Panic. Of course, it wasn't just the Fed that failed. Our system, both government and non-government, failed. In addition to the financial flaws discussed previously in this book, the stock market has another – Hedge Funds. Just why these Hedge Funds are dangerous is discussed. What should we do? The Chapter on Recommendations covers that. The very last chapter is a plea for Wall St. to return to its basics. Remember when Wall St. actually put its effort into investing in businesses that created wealth, productivity and jobs. That's what Wall St. needs to be doing instead of creatively making financial products like Synthetic Derivatives and Credit Default Swaps that add no value.

Chapter 11. The Fed Response

Exec Summary: The Fed failed to do any type of failure analysis when Bear Stearns failed, and its failure was repeated. The Fed still has not done any failure analysis today (as this book has done). The Fed had an opportunity to demonstrate great financial leadership and failed.

How well did the Treasury/Fed Respond?

Neither the Treasury nor the Fed caused [T1-1] the Wall St. Panic of 2008. However, let me address the question of, "How well did they respond?" I would grade them a solid **"C"**. They did prevent a repeat of the Great Depression. However, they did not do the analysis of the effect of Subprime Mortgage failures and why Bear Stearns failed. Had they done this, they could have taken steps to prevent the Panic. We still would have had a Recession but not a Panic. The Panic led to a $700 Billion TARP bailout and the $800 Billion Stimulus Package. If we had suffered only a Recession, we would not have suffered as many unemployed or the government intervention in so many of our banks and companies.

Nevertheless, the Treasury/Fed did save us from another Depression. I would like to thank them before I spend the rest of the Chapter criticizing them. I have not lived through a Depression, but the previous generation in my family and that of my wife did. Here are a couple of stories from that time period.

A West Virginia Story from the Depression

My mother's family grew up in McMechen, West Virginia which is up in the panhandle in the coal and steel area of the greater Pittsburgh region. Her younger brother, my uncle Bill, always walked to school down the same streets and turned at one particular corner. A couple of older kids from his school lived in the corner house. One day on his way to school, he came to his turn, and the house was no longer there. It was just a pile of rubble. The father, a coal miner, brought home some dynamite and blew up his entire family (probably lost his job). Times were tough.

An Iowa Story from the Depression
When my father-in-law was 12 years old, his father died. His mother pulled him out of the one room school house to help her try and save the farm which is why he had only a 6th grade education. They didn't make it. His Mom took his sister and moved into town to work as a seamstress, but she couldn't support him so he went to work on a relative's farm in the middle of Nebraska. He worked for room and board and no money at all. Of course, he came home to be with his Mom at Christmas in Burlington, Iowa (located at the extreme southeast corner of Iowa). Getting to and from Burlington was a challenge since he had no money. He hitchhiked. Of course, hitch hiking across Iowa and half of Nebraska took a couple of days, and rides weren't plentiful. He took a pack with a half dozen sandwiches and a thermos of hot coffee. Frequently, he was stuck at night out in the open. For those unfamiliar with the weather in Iowa at Christmas, it was cold. It could easily be 0 degrees Fahrenheit and even lower with the wind chill factor. Now he wasn't some cream puff city slicker. He was a tough Iowa farm boy so he knew what to expect. He had 5 layers of pants, 5 layers of sweater/jackets, gloves and mittens. Nevertheless, lying in a ditch at the side of the road before hitch hiking the next morning wasn't fun. Times were tough.

Again, I would like to thank Mr. Paulson and Mr. Bernanke for making sure that we did not go into another Depression.

Response and Criticism

The rest of this Chapter is divided into two Sections. Section 11.1 will go over the Fed Response to the Bear, Lehman and AIG failures. Section 11.2 will discuss just two topics in criticizing the response: (1) The failure analysis that wasn't done (this book has done a Magic + 1 failure analysis) and (2) Why great financial leadership (grade **A**) could have saved the situation and avoided a Panic. We still would have had a Recession, of course. *For simplicity, instead of referring to the Treasury/Fed combination, I will just refer to the Fed. Both were involved, of course* [11-2].

11.1 The Fed Response to the Bear Stearns Failure

The Treasury/Fed Response when Bear Stearns failed in March 2008 was to get another bank to take it over. In this case, the Fed lent JP Morgan $30 Billion in order to do the takeover.

The Fed Response to the Lehman and AIG Failures

In the same week of September 2008, both Lehman Brothers and AIG failed. Lehman failed first followed by AIG a couple of days later. Did the Lehman failure trigger the AIG failure? Since we have almost no information disclosed about AIG, we can only speculate. My guess is that there was a connection. Lehman failed because it assets dropped in value (those good old Opaque Derivatives embedded with Subprimes) which triggered the withdrawal of its massive Overnight Lending. Basically, Lehman failed for Financial Causes (1) and (2). While the Fed tried to get a consortium of Wall St. banks to save Lehman, it was unwilling to make a loan as it did in the case of Bear Stearns. This caused Lehman to declare bankruptcy.

AIG failed primarily due to Financial Cause (3) CDS. It had issued CDS insurance which paid off in the event of failure of the insured Derivative or Company. In fact, AIG had to come up with collateral (e.g., cash) for its customers if the insured Derivative or Company or AIG had its rating downgraded. Since AIG had nowhere near the cash to back up its CDS insurance promises, it failed and was taken over by the government. I'll bet they didn't have $20 Billion on hand to handle claims, and the government AIG bailout was $180 Billion which gives some idea of how far off they were from reality. Now AIG was an insurance company and not a bank and not really under the purview of the Fed. Nevertheless, it seemed that if AIG failed, a number of major banks might also fail. If these banks could not count on AIG paying CDS insurance claims on the failing assets these banks held, there could be a string of failures.

Frankly, I suspect that the problems associated with AIG contributed more to the Panic than Lehman. AIG's role deserves a detailed book, but it is tough to write one when all the information is kept secret. If AIG went into bankruptcy as Lehman did, we would have far more information. I suspect that the Fed took over AIG to prevent this information from being made public.

11.2 Criticism of the Fed Response
There are so many aspects of the Fed's response to the failure of Bear and Lehman to criticize. I will confine my criticisms to just two areas: (1) Lack of Failure Analysis and (2) Missing the opportunity for great leadership.

11.2.1 Lack of Failure Analysis
What this book has tried to do is analyze what were the principal reasons for the Wall St. Panic of 2008. This type of thinking seems to be nearly entirely missing in the world of finance. Has anyone read the Fed report on why the Wall St. Panic happened? (I don't think one exists.) Has anyone read a book by the financial media describing the

top 3 reasons why we had a Financial Panic? There are certainly plenty of books reporting "what" happened, but I really can't recall any addressing "why". I haven't seen any analysis by the Fed or Treasury. This book may not be perfect or complete, but at least it offers up three reasons why the Panic occurred. This one man effort is better than what the 21,000 people at the Fed have managed to come up with.

Medical Failure Analysis
Failure Analysis is done in the medical field. When someone dies, there is an autopsy. If people start dying from Swine Flu, then there is a pathology analysis by the Centers for Disease Control (CDC). This analysis will allow an antidote to the Swine Flu to be developed (e.g, H1N1 flu shot). The objective is to mitigate a problem or even eliminate it. Does the financial world see something wrong with this approach? Or maybe our financial world is populated by people missing the "Failure Analysis" gene.

Aircraft Safety and Failure Analysis
Of course, I came from the aircraft industry. I'm pretty proud of the passenger aircraft safety record. Now flying is not 100% safe, but you probably have a better chance of being killed on your drive to the airport than flying across country. This didn't just happen. It is the result of a very thorough "analysis" of every aircraft accident in which the results are fed back into the system so the same accident will not occur again. One of my jobs was to help analyze the crash of a DC-8 aircraft on a training flight in New Orleans. What is important is not the aerodynamics involved. What's important is the methodology. We had a crash (like a financial crash). We gathered data. We analyzed the data. We determined the causes of the crash. We fed the results back into the aerospace industry so

another crash due to the same causes would not happen again.

Did the Fed analyze the failure of Bear so that an identical failure would not occur later with Lehman? No. What they did is what I call "The Bolivian Approach".

The Bolivian Approach

Years ago one of our Douglas engineers was in Bolivia on business. He was catching a flight north on a two engine propeller plane of some Bolivian Airline. As the pilot started the engines, the Douglas engineer noticed a considerable amount of smoke coming from the right engine. Then the pilot came out of the cockpit and argued with an airline manager at the door. Since the Douglas engineer didn't understand Spanish well, he asked the stewardess if she could tell from the argument how long the flight would be delayed to change the engine. She smiled and said there would be no delay at all. They were simply going to change the pilot.

Isn't "The Bolivian Approach" what was used for Bear Stearns? The Fed didn't attempt to correct Financial Cause (1) Balance Sheet Abuse or Financial Cause (2) Opaque Derivatives. It just changed pilots from Bear management to JP Morgan management. Not surprisingly, Lehman crashed 6 months later due to the same identical reasons. In the case of Lehman, the pilots were changed from Lehman management to the Bankruptcy Court. After Lehman failure, no failure analysis and corrective actions were taken (in terms of rule changes). The Bolivians would have approved. The Fed did flood the system with liquidity which raised the equity positions of every major bank. This did effectively take care of Financial Cause 1 (a) although without a permanent rule change.

11.2.2 Missing the opportunity for great leadership
Could the Fed have risen to greatness during September 2008 and prevented a Panic? Yes. The size of the Subprime problem that Wall St. faced was not so big that it should have caused Panic. When panicked financial media publications wrote that there were $5 Trillion in toxic assets in the market, the Fed could have countered with a credible estimate of the Subprime problem (as I have in Appendix 5. "Size of Subprimes"), acknowledge that a few thinly capitalized investment banks were in a tenuous financial position, but that the financial sector as a whole had the capital to absorb these problems as I illustrate in Appendix 8 "Bank Capital and Subprime Losses". There would have been no need for TARP although it would probably have been necessary for Merrill Lynch to merge and Morgan Stanley and Goldman Sachs to transform themselves into normal banks.

Figure 11.1

The reason for Appendix 5. "Size of Subprimes" is to provide a Ball Park estimate for the size of the Subprime problem on Wall St. Remember that half my estimate of $400 Billion of Subprime losses went to Fannie/Freddie ($200 Billion) who had already been bailed out by the government to the tune of $180 Billion. This meant that the remaining $200 Billion of Subprime loss could be in Wall St. or other banks. Probably a good portion of that loss had already been recognized by September of 2008. My estimates are in the table below:

Recognized Bank Subprime Losses	
Bank	Loss ($ Bil)
Bear Stearns failure	30
Lehman failure	30
Merrill Lynch merger	30
Other banks	30
Total	120

Table 11.1

Let's recall that other non-Wall St. banks that held Subprimes also failed during the 2006-2008 time period. These include Countrywide, Indymac, Washington Mutual and Wachovia. If the estimates in Table 11.1 are correct or even close, then the remaining stronger banks of Wall St. were facing perhaps $80 Billion in losses vs. their $800 Billion in equity. In Appendix 8. "Bank Capital and Subprime Losses", I discuss this subject in more detail. With the Fed ready to lend cash for collateral for all normal banks (which the investment banks had transformed themselves into), there should have been no Panic. There should have been no necessity for TARP, no Stimulus Package, no government intervention in our banking system. An opportunity for greatness was missed. We needed a J. Pierpont Morgan and didn't have one.

Summary

Could the Fed have prevented a Panic? Absolutely yes. First, the Fed failed to do any kind of failure analysis and feed the results back into the financial system. If just Financial Cause (1) Balance Sheet Abuse had been corrected for Lehman, it is probable that we would have merely had a Recession instead of a Panic. The Fed could have converted Lehman into a normal bank as it later did with Morgan Stanley and Goldman Sachs. What a costly missed opportunity. It was probably the worst financial decision since the 1929 Depression.

Second, as the financial system teetered on the brink of Panic, the Fed failed the greatness test. It could have estimated the extent of the Subprime failures as I did in Appendix 5, estimated the portion of these failures that found their way to Wall St., estimated the losses incurred thus far and deduced the size of the remaining failures. The size of the remaining Subprime failures was small compared to the size of Wall St.'s capital as shown in Table 11.1 and Appendix 8. The Fed could have stated this authoritatively and nipped the Panic in the bud. It failed.

98

Chapter 12. Failure at all Levels

Exec Summary: It wasn't just the Fed that failed. Nearly every level failed. The self regulators as well as the government failed.

Did just Wall St. fail and cause the Panic of 2008? No, it was failure at nearly all levels. Let me make some brief comments on the failures of many of the participants.

Wall St. Banks
This book has described the three principal reasons why the Wall St. system failed and caused a Panic. Wall St.'s grade is "F".

The Fed/Treasury
The Fed did not fail completely. It did save us from a Depression. It gets a grade of "C" for that effort. However, the Fed completely failed to do any failure analysis. It deserves a grade of "F" for no failure analysis. It completely failed to stem a Panic when no Panic was really justified. It had more information, more insight into every bank than any other organization in the country. Yet, with all this knowledge, it failed to stop the Panic. Furthermore, the Fed has not told the American people "the whole truth" about AIG. The Fed has raised no warning flags on $600 Trillion of Derivatives (99% unregulated) and $30 Trillion of CDS (100% unregulated). My grade for its overall effort is "D".

Regulator: SEC
This organization is pathetic. The SEC allowed the investment banks to drop to only 2% capitalization. It dropped the uptick rule [12-1]. It couldn't discover the $50 Billion Ponzi Scheme of Bernie Madoff. Grade "F-". Mary Schapiro gets an "A" for bringing the Abacus Case

against Goldman Sachs. We have one smart woman leading a herd of incompetents.

Regulator: CFTC

This regulator shows that there is some hope for government regulation. It has regulated its derivatives successfully. Grade "A-".

Regulator: FDIC

This regulator also shows that there is some hope for government regulation. The prime duty of the FDIC is to protect the money of people who deposit their savings at a bank. Many of these banks have failed. The Depositors have not lost their money. Grade "A".

Self Regulator: Rating Agencies

Standard and Poors, Moody's and Fitch initially gave the Mortgage Backed Derivatives high credit ratings. These Derivatives were dangerous, prone to failure and did not deserve these ratings. How can anyone in their right mind agree that some portion of Subprimes deserve AAA ratings? The Rating Agencies did downgrade their initial ratings when it became obvious how high the Subprime failure rate was. Grade "D".

Rating Agencies for FICO [12-2]

Trans Union, Experian and EquiFax gave low FICO scores to the Subprime borrowers. They were right. They did their job. They were ignored. Grade "A".

Congress

Congress pushed the Subprime borrowing program with vigor and intimidation. This is absolutely the worst program in history. It has been 1 ½ years since the Panic of 2008. Congress has done no meaningful investigation. It has finally started the Financial Crisis Inquiry Commission (not to be confused with true Failure Analysis). Congress has passed no financial reforms to correct the three Financial Causes and Bad Input discussed in this book. The Dodd Bill is under discussion as this book is being written. I make a comparison between the Dodd Bill and my Recommendations in Chapter 14. Even if it is passed, the Dodd Bill will not prevent another Panic. Congress deserves a grade of "F".

Business Schools
Now I realize that some of the leaders of Wall St. banks did not even have an MBA. Nevertheless, there are plenty of them on Wall St. Their absolute disregard for investing in growth, jobs and productivity instead of non-productive junk such as most Derivatives and all CDS, makes one wonder what they are teaching in Business Schools. Does MBA stand for Master's in Business Administration or Maximizing Bonus Acquisition? Furthermore, where is any intelligent analysis by a Business School on the Wall St. Panic of 2008? Grade "F".

Financial Media
Where is our financial media? It should always be our first line of defense. It should be our watchdog. All our financial media seems capable of is doing an interview and repeating back what was told to them. Where's the thinking? Where's the analysis? Where's the focus on productivity? Are they watchdogs or parrots just repeating? Grade "F".

Accounting Boards
It doesn't take an edict from Congress to act. The Accounting Boards, both domestic and international, have the power to act. They can change the rules from 2% capitalization to 8% capitalization. They can change the rules on how much Overnight Lending is allowed. They

can change the rules on showing the risk of CDS insurance losses on Balance Sheets. Grade "F".

Grassroots Level

When nearly every other level has failed, it is up to the grassroots level. The grassroots may not think they have the power, but every once and awhile they show such as the election of Senator Scott Brown in Massachusetts. It's time to take our country and financial system back. Grade "TBD".

Chapter 13. Hedge Funds

Exec Summary: **Hedge Funds are completely unregulated. They need regulation in at least two areas: (1) allowable leverage and (2) ultra fast trading.**

Definition: Hedge Fund

A Hedge Fund is a means of investment like a Mutual Fund on steroids. It is secret and unregulated. There are no limits on the leverage it may use. This leverage could be 100 to 1 which means that the Hedge Fund could borrow $100 from banks for each $1 dollar its investment members contribute. These Hedge Funds file no public accounting statements so we can only guess at what they do. Hedge Funds engage in ultra fast trading. Hedge Funds probably control $2 Trillion of our $10 Trillion stock market and perhaps 75% of the trading volume. Hedge Funds are limited to 100 investors who can invest at least $1 million.

This section may be a little tough for many readers to follow. Terms like ultra fast trading, portfolio insurance, buying long and selling short may be a little intimidating. Don't worry. There is no test at the end of the Chapter. Just keep reading. I think you will come away with the idea that Hedge Funds can really determine much of what is happening in our stock market (or perhaps a more accurate description would be "their market).

Ultra Fast Trading on May 6, 2010

In a 15 minute period, the Dow Jones Average dropped 1,000 points or about 10% of its total value. A major company, Accenture, dropped from a stock price of $40/share to 1 cent/share. This should worry everyone. Is this a stock market that is reflecting reality or is this a stock market that is being jerked around by an unseen force? Well, there was no particular news event that happened in that 15 minute period (such as war being declared). Therefore, it seems like some unseen force was acting on the market.

Now the SEC is investigating but has come up with no conclusions. In my opinion, we are asking a bunch of lawyers to solve a mathematical problem, and the chances of them doing that are pretty low. What the SEC needs to do is subcontract out the math analysis to one or more mathematical competent organizations such as universities, major computer firms or engineering companies.

My guess is that the market was plunged on its downward spiral by the ultra fast algorithmic (formula) programs of the Hedge Funds. These programs connect directly to the trading markets and can execute trades in less than one thousandth of a second. In fact, the time can be 16 microseconds or more than 6,000 times/second.

There are two aspects of this ultra fast or flash trading that should be noted. The first is that this ultra fast trading accounts for something like 75% of the daily market volume. If these programs are accounting for 75% of the trading volume, they are essentially setting the price of the stocks. Now can I prove this? No, I don't have access to the trading data. But if a major company's stock can go from $40 to 1 cent in 15 minutes, I have a sneaking suspicion that I am right. If any decent mathematical organization did an analysis of the trading in Accenture's stock for those 15 minutes, it would probably confirm that I am right.

The second aspect of this ultra fast trading is that it is based on algorithms or formulas. Now we don't know what these formulas are, but it is likely that they are based on the fluctuations observed in market prices. In other words, they may see the price of a particular stock go down, and the program is set to react to this price decrease by selling that stock (or selling it short[13-1]). If a bunch of these programs have similar programming formulas, it would be possible to drive Accenture's stock to 1 cent. Now I am certainly not able to prove my assertions, but I think it is a pretty good theory. If it looks like a duck, quacks like a duck, it is probably a duck.

Now in the olden days when I first was in the stock market 44 years ago, stock prices were largely determined by news events. For example, if Boeing won a contract, its stock price went up. If it lost the contract, its stock price went down. These ultra fast trading programs are different. They don't care about news. What they are focused on is price fluctuations. I don't even think they care about what stocks they are trading. They are just looking for fluctuations and getting in and out in 16 microseconds. (Of course, I could be wrong and find out that some stock trader is just a really fast thinker and can make 6,000 decisions in 1 second.) One of the questions we should be asking ourselves is if we want our market to act like that. Another question is, "How well is the market representing reality (e.g., Accenture worth 1 cent)?"

October 1987

One day in October 1987, the stock market dropped 25%. The Brady Commission investigated this and concluded that it was due to "portfolio management". What was "portfolio management"? No one knows exactly because it was secret. It was programmed trading. Basically the idea was that you could protect your investment if you simultaneously bought long and sold short the same stocks. Another key ingredient was the high leverage of Hedge Funds which probably varied between 20 to 1 and 100 to 1. Now any real attempt at explaining "portfolio insurance" is beyond the Magic +1 level of this book. For those interested, please read "A Demon of our own Design" by Bookstaber.

Definition: Margin Call
An ordinary investor like me can buy a stock with my money and also a loan from the brokerage I am dealing with. This loan from the brokerage is called Margin. As a result of the Great Depression, I am limited to 50% Margin. In other words if I buy a stock for $100, I will have to put up $50 of my money and can borrow $50 from the brokerage. However, I have to protect the $50 borrowed from the brokerage. If my stock drops to $80, I have to make up the $20 difference. This is termed a Margin Call. Hedge Funds have no 50% margin limit. They can buy a $100 with $1 of their money and $99 borrowed.

What probably happened on that fateful day in October when the stock market dropped 25% is that one Hedge Fund's investment suffered a loss, and it had to cover its Margin Call so it had to sell another stock. For example, let's say the Hedge Fund A owned GE at a price of 100 and was leveraged 100 to 1. GE loses a contract and drops to 90. Now this is a problem for the Hedge Fund because it is borrowed $99 to purchase the GE stock. It needs to raise $10 to meet its margin call. Therefore Hedge Fund A sells a sizeable amount of another of its stocks, say IBM. Now this Hedge Fund is also leveraged 100 to 1 in IBM so it has to sell quite a bit to raise the $10. Well, as it so happens, Hedge Fund B owns IBM, and the sale of that stock by Hedge Fund A drives the price of IBM down which means Hedge Fund B has to meet a margin call and must sell another stock, and the downward spiral of Hedge Fund sales began. It ended up with the market 25% lower. It was leverage, leverage, leverage.

1998 Long Term Capital Management
Long Term Capital Management (LTCM) was a very secretive and successful Hedge Fund. It routinely returned gains of 40% a year which means anyone invested with them would be doubling their money in just two years. How did it do this? A good description is given in "When Genius Failed: The Rise and Fall of Long Term Capital Management" by Lowenstein. One of the ingredients of LTCM's success was very high leverage which was 100 to 1 at the end. Remember in Chapter 7 on Leverage, I said that **Leverage cuts both ways**. Well, leverage certainly helped LTCM make 40% returns, but the Russians defaulted on their debt in 1998, and this had a very adverse effect on LTCM because of its leverage. In a matter of weeks, its losses were so great that it needed a $3 Billion bailout by Wall St. Banks. This was orchestrated by Fed Chairman Greenspan because a failure of LTCM could have seriously disrupted the stock market as Lehman's failure did. LTCM had approximately $1 Billion in capital, $130 Billion in bank loans and $1.4 Trillion in Derivatives. It was leverage, leverage, leverage.

Black Swan Event
Seeing a Black Swan is rare. This term is used to describe some event that might only happen once in 10,000 years. This is how LTCM strategized its trading. Unfortunately, a Black Swan (Bad Input) in the form of a Russian Default ruined their plan. Subprimes were another Black Swan. It turns out these Black Swans are not really so rare. See further discussion in Appendix 10. "Black Swans".

Summary
Hedge Funds are totally unregulated. Only when one fails, such as LTCM, do we have any insight into how they operate. Hedge Funds are highly leveraged, and there are no rules limiting the amount of their leverage. Even though

Hedge Funds are merely a collection of wealthy investors, they are not limited to 50% margin like you or me. Hedge Funds engage in ultra fast trading and are dominating the stock market today. If a Black Swan event (e.g., Greek Debt Default, Euro collapse, China selling US Treasuries) occurs, Hedge Funds could cause another Wall St. Panic.

Financial Cause (4) Hedge Funds

Chapter 14. Recommendations

Exec Summary: I will just limit myself to 7 recommendations and a comparison with the Dodd Bill (and self regulators).

Recommendations

1. Restraining Order

There should be a restraining order against the creation of any further non-regulated Derivatives and CDS insurance. This would at least limit further damage while these issues are investigated in detail. There should be a restraining order on 2% capitalization and massive Overnight Lending. These restraining orders should have been put into effect with the failure of Bear Stearns in March 2008. They are long overdue.

2. Gather Data

The first step required to analyze and fix any problem is to gather data. The American people need:

(a) <u>Subprimes</u>

We need the complete set of data on the number of failures. I believe this is being deliberately withheld from the Public.

(b) <u>$600 Trillion of Derivatives</u>

What are these based on? Which companies/entities own them? Do they show up on Balance Sheets? How does $600 Trillion correlate to a $14 Trillion GDP????

(c) <u>$30 Trillion of CDS</u>

How much CDS is out there? How much capital is there set aside to pay off claims??? Does CDS show up on Balance Sheets? What does the remaining AIG CDS insure?

(d) <u>Hedge Funds</u>

What's their leverage? How much have they borrowed from banks? What percent of the daily trading volume do they represent?

3. Cause (1): Balance Sheet Abuse

I don't particularly care whether Congress, the SEC, the Fed or the Accounting Boards take the lead. Someone has got to do something. No bank should ever be allowed to have 2% capitalization. Neither should Fannie Mae or Freddie Mac. Change the stupid rule to 8% capitalization!! This doesn't take a genius or a lot of analysis (which I have already done). Now the reality is that by the investment banks transforming themselves into normal banks, this has been done, but we still need a rule change. There is some discussion of them transforming themselves back into investment banks.

There is no rule limiting Overnight Lending. The need to do so should be obvious to anyone that understands a Balance Sheet. Relying on Overnight Lending for 10% of your funding is crazy at such a fundamental level. Limit Overnight Lending to 1% of the capital structure of any bank or company.

4. Cause (2): Derivatives

All Derivatives are not bad as I have described with the Futures regulated by the CFTC. But the Subprime Derivatives were terrible unless a $5 Trillion loss in the stock market and 10% unemployment doesn't bother you. Do we know whether or not some other malicious Derivative(s) are out there? No we don't. Some country (like Greece) could default on its debt. This would probably make interest rates spike upward which would affect interest rate swaps. The result could be another Panic (on interest rate Derivatives not Subprimes, of course) [14-1].

Anything as huge as $600 Trillion has to be investigated and made transparent. It's been 1 ½ years since the Panic of 2008. Do we want another?

5. Cause (3): Credit Default Swaps (CDS)
Subprime Mortgages may have totaled between $1.3 and $2 Trillion. Their losses are probably between $400 -750 Billion thus far. The loss from CDS insurance on just Subprimes and related issues is probably $180 Billion (the size of the AIG bailout). Yet, there is $30 Trillion of CDS insurance out there. We have no idea what it is insuring. There could be another financial disaster such as Interest Rate Derivatives just waiting to happen and have its effect multiplied by CDS losses. We have no idea how much capital there is to pay off further CDS insurance claims although it can't be even close to $30 Trillion. To put this number in perspective, the whole European Union is struggling to come up with a $1 Trillion superfund to back up the Euro. Even this superfund could not pay off all CDS. What we do know is that CDS insurance is a gambling device where the holder of the insurance can receive a pay out even if he doesn't suffer a loss. CDS is a more flawed product than even Subprimes, and that's saying something. When we have a dangerous toy or any type of bad product, we recall it. It is time to recall CDS. Have the issuers of CDS reimburse the buyers of CDS their premiums to the extent they can and terminate the CDS product!!!

6. Cause (4): Hedge Funds
Regulate Hedge Funds. Hedge Funds are nothing but collections of individuals. One of the purposes of Hedge Funds is to get around the 50% margin rule that the rest of us peons that invest in the stock market have to abide by. Margin borrowing of 50% of our investment essentially limits ordinary citizens to a leverage of 2 to 1. Yet we

know that the Hedge Fund of LTCM had leverage of 100 to 1. Did someone designate Hedge Fund participants as super citizens that are allowed more leverage than I or you are allowed? If so, I didn't get the memo. It is time to regulate Hedge Funds and make them report publicly just like Mutual Funds do. Not only are Hedge Funds highly leveraged, *__every dollar they borrow from banks is one less dollar for American businesses that invest in growth not gambling.__*

7. Failure Analysis

The NTSB does failure analysis on every airplane crash. We need a similar function performed in our financial system. Yes, I realize that there is a Financial Crisis Inquiry Commission, but the end result of this will probably be some general, qualitative summary. What we need is in-depth quantitative analysis. For example, we need to know how many Subprimes failed. What was the correlation with FICO score and no downpayment? How many Subprime Mortgage Derivatives failed? What is the correlation between ownership of CDS on Subprimes with the actual ownership of the Subprime Derivatives? How does having 10% of a company's debt financed by Overnight Lending affect its vulnerability. These are just some of the parameters that need to be quantified.

It is obvious that when Bear Stearns collapsed, the lack of a failure analysis and corrective actions led directly to the collapse of Lehman for essentially the same reasons. This is unacceptable.

In my opinion, none of our governmental agencies (SEC, CFTC, Treasury, Fed) have the necessary mathematical tools and skills necessary to address the quantitative aspects of failure analysis. Frankly, I think the NTSB could probably do a better job than any of them. However, I think what really should be done is to utilize the skills available to us at universities, computer firms (e.g. IBM, Control Data) and engineering firms (e.g., Boeing, Lockheed). The governmental agencies should contract the quantitative failure analysis work out to these national resources that do have the math and analytical skills to do the necessary analysis. We need to analyze both past failures and potential future failures (see Appendix 10. "Black Swans").

Observation

1. Bonuses – the symptom not the disease

It is politically attractive to attack the Wall St. bonus system. However, I would attack it a different way than taxing the bonuses. The bonuses come from commissions on selling Trillions of Derivatives and CDS. I would eliminate the Derivatives (not all of them) and CDS (all of them). If the Trillions disappear so will the huge commissions and therefore the huge bonuses. Nail the disease not the symptom.

Comparing the Dodd Bill vs. My Recommendations

Comparison of the Dodd Bill to My Recommendations	
My Recommendations	Dodd Bill
1. Restraining order	0
2. Gather Data	0.1
3. Cause (1) Balance Sheet Abuse	0
4. Cause (2) Derivatives	0.5
5. Cause (3) Credit Default Swaps (CDS)	0
6. Cause (4) Hedge Funds	0
7. Failure Analysis	0.1

Table 14.1

At the time of this writing, the Dodd Bill is still going through Congress. Table 14.1 is based on my guess of its outcome. As you can see, I don't think the Dodd Bill will prevent the next Panic. Let me just discuss the few areas where the Dodd Bill and my Recommendations resonate a bit. In the Dodd Bill, there is supposed to be some small office in the Treasury that sort of looks at Failure Analysis. First, I think this office will be small, weak and not have the right skill set to do the job. Second, while science and the NTSB are objective, economics is partisan. I think it would be better to contract this work out to many different resources in this country (and see if their results agree). On "Gather Data", I will have to say that at least Congress formed the Financial Crisis Inquiry Commission. However, much more needs to be done.

In the area of Derivatives, the Dodd Bill might take some important steps in the right direction. The most important and valuable piece of the entire bill is the Volcker Rule. This would separate banks from proprietary trading and Derivatives (or essentially gambling). In the next Panic, the banks that actually lend to people and businesses would be left standing. The subsidiaries that deal in Derivatives could fail without affecting the economy as much. The second encouraging step is forcing most (it should be all) Derivatives through a Clearinghouse. This will allow some transparency although more should be done.

The most glaring omissions of the Dodd Bill are:

(1) The complete failure to ban CDS. The issue of "insurable interest" isn't even mentioned. There is no requirement to put CDS risk on the Balance Sheet.

(2) Hedge Funds are not addressed at all. Clearly they have the most effective lobbyists of all. They don't have to register. There is no limitation on the amount of leverage they can use. There is no limit on their ultra fast trading which gives them another form of leverage over the market.

(3) Balance Sheet Abuse. There is no limitation on Overnight Lending. There is no explicit regulation for 8% capitalization.

(4) Failure Analysis. There is no plan for thorough quantitative failure analysis using all of our national resources.

Comparison: Recommendations & Accounting Boards
I don't want to just criticize the Dodd Bill and Congress. Certainly, they could do a better job, but our self regulators could do much better as well. In fact, if our self regulators were doing a better job, Congress would have to do less which is the method I would prefer.

Let me address My Recommendations dealing with the 4 Financial Causes I identify and what one self regulator, the Accounting Boards could do.

Financial Cause (1) Balance Sheet Abuse
The Accounting Boards could decide that all banks need a capitalization of 8%. They could decide that overnight lending was limited to 1% of asset value.

Financial Cause (2) Opaque Derivatives
Accounting Boards could insist that all Derivatives appear on Balance Sheets with appropriate footnotes.

Financial Cause (3) Credit Default Swaps (CDS)

Accounting Boards could insist that some portion of the potential loss from CDS insurance (e.g., 10%) show up on Balance Sheets with a footnote specifying the maximum potential pay out loss.

Financial Cause (4) Hedge Funds

Accounting Boards could insist that all Hedge Fund Balance Sheets be public knowledge. They could insist that all banks that lend to Hedge Funds clearly state how much money is lent to Hedge Funds (vs. simply shown as a loan).

My point is that implementation of My Recommendations or similar reforms can be done both by Congress and the private sector.

Addendum

The best regulation tool we have is the "freedom to fail". While we would love for every company to succeed, this is just not how it works out. Stagecoaches pulled by horses were replaced by cars, trains and airplanes. This is the "creative destruction" described by Schumpeter at work. It is a system that constantly lets the best company rise to the top.

However, the Greek admonition, "nothing in excess", applies to failure also. The Great Depression was a gigantic failure, but it was not a good way to regulate. When the failure is too big, it is counterproductive.

We have $600 Trillion of Derivatives and $30 Trillion of CDS. There is absolutely no way our system can absorb large failures in these two categories. The solution is pretty simple. They have to be shrunk in size. CDS should be eliminated entirely. The $600 Trillion in Derivatives should end up being less that the size of our GDP at $14 Trillion and should be 100% regulated.

Chapter 15. What's the Value Added?

Up to this point, this book identified and analyzed the basic causes of the Panic of 2008 plus my concern about Hedge Funds. In summary they are:

Bad Input: Subprimes
Financial Cause (1): Balance Sheet Abuse (leverage)
Financial Cause (2): Opaque Mortgage Derivatives
Financial Cause (3): Credit Default Swaps
Financial Cause (4): Hedge Funds

In this Chapter, my approach will be different. I want to examine some of the creative finance products (e.g, Derivatives, Credit Default Swaps) and ask a more basic question:

What's the Value Added?

Who should be asking this question? Everyone. It should start with our business schools. Our financial media should be our watchdog and be asking this question. Our business leaders should be asking this question, especially in the banking sector. Our Congress, our regulators and everyone else ought to be asking this question. The only person that is asking this question is Paul Volcker who was the head of the Fed which pulled us out of the decade long inflation of the 1970s. This should be the first question asked when money is invested. This should be the first question asked when capital is allocated.

What's the Value Added?
This basic concept seems to have eluded many of our bankers on Wall St. I understood it when I was in the 5th grade. My Dad had explained how the stock market worked to me.

A game of marbles, Wall St. and Las Vegas

When I was in the 5th grade, we used to play marbles before class. One day I was playing a game with my friend Bob, and I mentioned that my Dad invested in the stock market. Bob said that his Dad wouldn't because it was just like gambling. I told him that was wrong. Yes, both gambling and investing both shared risk, but gambling never produced anything. You could play 10 games of poker, but no airplane was built or no house constructed. Essentially, no value was added. However, if you invested in Douglas Aircraft, planes would be built. Instead of driving for days to go back East, we could fly in one day. Essentially, value was added. The difference between gambling and investing is not risk. It is in the value added.

Today, Bob's Dad may have been closer to the truth than my Dad. With $600 Trillion in Derivatives and $30 Trillion in CDS, Wall St. resembles Las Vegas more than a capitalist investment machine.

Huge bonuses are paid on Wall St. not for investing in the next Apple Computer Company or the next Amazon. They are paid for selling a $Trillion of repackaged mortgages. Others are paid huge bonuses for promising to have their CDS insurance pay off in the event of failure and still getting those bonuses even when the insurance doesn't pay off. Or some Hedge Fund manager can get a $20 Billion pay off from CDS insurance when he doesn't even have a loss to be compensated for. All this is done in the name of creative finance and laissez faire. Come on. Give me a break.

This isn't putting lipstick on a pig. It is putting lipstick on a snake.

Figure 15.1

The correlation between huge Wall St. bonuses and value added just isn't there. Now is the problem big income? No. Bill Gates has a big income. The problem is big income with no value added. Let me contrast Wall St. with Silicon Valley.

Silicon Valley

David Packard and Steve Jobs started their businesses in different garages in Palo Alto. Packard's company turned into HP. Jobs' company turned into Apple. Have these companies added value? You bet. Between them, HP and Apple make excellent personal computers, printers, IPODs and other products that make us more productive and America more productive. Their companies have created thousands of jobs. David Packard and Steve Jobs deserve to be Billionaires. They added value.

Let's contrast this with the hedge fund manager that made $20 Billion because he held the right CDS contracts. Did he add value with new computers, IPODs or any other product? No. Did he create thousands of jobs even though he nearly made as much as Bill Gates of Microsoft? No. What he did was make a ton of money while adding absolutely no value. The difference between him and a gambler in Las Vegas winning $20 Billion at a roulette wheel is absolutely nothing. They are both gamblers. They both add no value.

Capitalism gets off track every so often. Capitalism is the greatest tool for the material improvement of mankind. But every so often, capitalism gets off track and needs a course correction. Let me briefly discuss three "off track" events

Capitalism gets off track with the Trusts
Between the end of the Civil War and World War I was a period of tremendous economic growth for the US. However, it became apparent that at the beginning of the century, too much power was concentrated in the hands of a few large Trusts such as Standard Oil. It is not as though these Trusts were adding no value. They were, but they were developing into monopolies or oligopolies (domination by just a few companies). Our country realized that *competition* was critical to our growth. Therefore, it established Anti-Trust Laws that were designed to optimize competition and minimize monopolies. Our capitalism which was getting off track in the direction of monopolies was put back on the right track to competition.

Capitalism gets off track in 1929

In 1929, our capitalism got off track for another reason – excessive leverage. The whole process of the Great Depression is extremely complex, and I certainly will not try to address all aspects. I will just concentrate on the excessive leverage. Individual investors were allowed to buy stocks with only 5% down. When the stock market rose too far and corrected downward, these investors were wiped out which in turn led to stock brokerages failing and other cascading failures. The corrective action with regard to individual shareholders was to require them to put at least 50% down. This measure and other steps got our capitalism back on track.

Capitalism gets off track in 2008

It became apparent that our capitalism was off track again in 2008. However, the contributing causes had been occurring throughout the first years of the 21st century. In my opinion, our capitalism got off track for two reasons: (1) the familiar excessive leverage which showed up this time in Subprime Mortgages and the Balance Sheets of Investment Banks and (2) the creative finance generation of $600 Trillion of Derivatives and $30 Trillion of CDS products which basically add no value. The corrective actions to get back on track are: (1) reduce the leverage (partially accomplished) and (2) get back to productive investments and ditch the non-productive ones. This is the basic task of allocating capital.

Allocating Capital

The capital allocated to HP, Apple, Amazon and Microsoft was obviously a wise allocation. We have received back a tremendous value added. The success of these companies is history, of course. Fortunately for us, American innovation is on-going. Even though it is tough to pick future successes, let me try to pick one.

Synthetic Genomics

This company is about 20 miles from where I live in San Diego. It is headed by Craig Ventner. Hopefully, that name is familiar. He played a key part in mapping the Human Genome and creating the first synthetic bacteria.

One of the main problems this country has is oil imports. If the price of oil goes up (as it did in 2008), it can have disastrous effects on our industries such as airlines and autos. In fact, the combination of a huge rise in gasoline prices plus a credit crunch as the result of the 2008 Panic annihilated 2 of our 3 largest auto companies. One approach to helping solve this oil/gas problem is to try and produce it from algae.

Unfortunately at the present time, the cost of producing gas from algae is about $20/gallon. One problem is that while algae produce oil, it is hard to separate it from the algae. Some people at General Atomics (in San Diego) think they can produce gas at $5/gallon using a chemical solvent process. The Synthetic Genomic approach is different. It isn't chemical. It's genetic. Ventner altered the genetic structure of his algae so they secrete the oil. Then it is a simple process to separate the oil from the water that the algae are in. There are more steps required, of course. The hope is that it just might be cost competitive. BP and Exxon have together invested a combined $900 Million with Ventner. Oh, now this is certainly chicken feed compared to $600 Trillion in Derivatives, but this investment just might "add value".

Imagine if these genetically altered algae produced gas at $3/gallon. As soon as we ramped up production, we wouldn't need to import any oil at all. We would need to build algae ponds all over our desert areas. The potential gas from algae per acre is 25 times more than ethanol from corn. That means if we had as many acres of algae ponds as we have acres for corn ethanol, we could satisfy our needs and even export oil. It would mean lots of jobs. It would be a renewable energy source. No more hunting for oil. If it works, it could be the greatest thing since the light bulb (which also came from America). Do a google search for: Synthetic Genomics.

Now there is absolutely no guarantee that gas from algae will be practical. But one thing is absolutely for certain. No money invested in Derivatives or CDS will ever produce any oil at all.

Summary
We have a mind boggling $600 Trillion in Derivatives. Various reasons are given why this is a good idea: it's risk management, it's securitization, it's laissez faire and it's creative finance. What we need to do with these $600 Trillion of Derivatives is to put them through a thorough "productivity audit". We need to ask:

"What's the Value Added?"

Chapter 16. Summary

The first objective of this book has been to illustrate that the Panic of 2008 was due to more than just the Subprime Mess. The second objective of this book has been to familiarize readers with the Magic + 1 level thesis for the Panic of 2008. These Financial Causes are: (1) Balance Sheet Abuse or Excessive Leverage, (2) Opaque Derivatives and (3) Credit Default Swaps. If these concepts are not clear, please re-read the appropriate Chapter(s). Please read Wikipedia, do a google search or read the appropriate books listed in the Bibliography.

The third objective of this book has been to remind Wall St. what the essence of capitalism is......Value Added. It is the process of creating growth, jobs and improving productivity. The essence of capitalism is not big bonuses or Derivatives.

The fourth objective of this book was to supply a simplified list of recommendations to change our system. Does this mean exclusively government imposed changes? No. The Self Regulators (Accounting Boards, Rating Services, Banks and others) should propose and implement changes in order to minimize the need for government regulation. At present, the Self Regulators are batting a big, fat zero.

Someone has to say that "The Emperor is wearing no clothes" even if that someone is me. A financial system that has a $14 Trillion GDP and $600 Trillion of Derivatives for risk management on this GDP is just operating in Financial Fantasyland. In 2008, we saw the effect of the Subprime Black Swan (Bad Input) on just $2 Trillion of this $600 Trillion monster. Our financial system crashed and brought the economy down with it. Do we really want to keep the other $598 Trillion of Derivatives secret and not see the light of day? Do we really want to risk a second Panic if a new and different Black Swan [16-1] sails into that Derivative system?

The choice for America and Wall St. is whether we want to follow the sign for "Big Bonuses and Derivatives" or the sign for "Value Added" investing.

Chapter Notes, Appendices, Bibliography, Glossary, Acronyms, Fact Table

Chapter Notes

2-1 References. I read a lot of financial publications including: Wall St. Journal, Investor's Business Daily, Financial Times, Barron's, Business Week, Forbes, Economist and more. From those publications, I have a general idea of the value of each financial parameters such as the size of real estate mortgages. Rather than quote 4 sources, I will quote none. However, I will refer the reader to Wikipedia which is the best single source in my opinion.

2-2 Other factors for Panic. The Housing Asset Bubble, Too big to fail, Fannie/Freddie, Off Balance Sheet Accounting, Short Selling, Rating Agencies, Repo Market, Rehypothecation and more. This book is just a Magic + 1 level discussion.

2-3 Secret info. Examples include the cumulative failure rate for Subprimes issued in 2005 & 2006. What is the remaining CDS of AIG issued on? Was there a connection between Lehman and AIG? The government is certainly not telling the public "The Whole Truth".

2-4 Address the critical issues even without complete info. Now obviously it would be better to have complete info, but sometimes the world is not that nice. You have to go with the info you have. This is fundamental to the approach taken in this book. For example, I don't know the exact size of the Subprime Failures, but it is a critical issue, and I must make a best estimate.

2-5 Emergency Landing. Our emergency was nothing compared to the "Miracle on the Hudson", but it was our's. Our instruments, starting with the artificial horizon, started to fail in extremely cloudy weather as we were flying over a swamp. Was our electrical system failing? Was our engine going to fail? We didn't know so we assessed our problem based on the knowledge we had and got the plane on the ground ASAP.

2-6 Black Box. This is not the Black Box that is retrieved from an airplane crash. This Black Box represents a complex system as a simple Black Box.

4-1 National Wealth. Of course, there are other elements that make up our national wealth than simply real estate and the stock market. However, these are the elements that are relevant to this book, and I will lump all other elements as "Other".

6-1 FICO = Fair Isaac Company. The score is an indication of credit worthiness.

6-2 Subprime Cumulative Failure Rate. It is extremely important for the US public to know what the cumulative failure rates for Subprimes are. For example, in 2005 there was a high volume of Subprime loans for home purchases made (the so-called NINJA loans). If we just assumed a uniform 15% failure rate each year from 2005 to 2010, you would have a cumulative failure rate of 75% (5 x 15%). Can you understand why Congress, HUD and the Fed would want to keep this secret? Some publications show a cumulative failure rate of 35%, but their data ends in 2007.

6-3 Subprimes for 2005, 2006. Why just these two years? First, these were the poorest quality Subprime loans known as NINJA loans. Second, the dollar volume of 2005-2006 approximately equaled all the previously issued Subprimes. Subprime issuance essentially stopped in early 2007.

7-1 Uptick Rule. The old uptick rule applied to short sales. Before you could make a short sale, the market had to tick up. Short sales are beyond the scope of this book.

7-2 Schapiro improvement. Under Mary Schapiro, the SEC brought the Abacus CDO case against Goldman Sachs. This is the first meaningful attempt at enforcement by the SEC in a decade.

9-1 AIG Derivatives. The AIG website, www.aigcorporate.com, gives the total value of Derivatives and Credit Default Swaps that AIG had from 9/08 thru 12/09. It originally had $390 Billion of CDS. It doesn't say whether AIG was the issuing party on these CDS, but that is likely. It also doesn't say what the CDS are insuring or who were the buyers.

9-2 $80 Billion Capital. My estimate is $80 Billion in Capital for the whole AIG company. Most of this capital would be allocated to its legitimate life and property insurance functions with very little for CDS. My guess is $20 Billion max for CDS pay outs or collateral calls.

9-3 Goldman pay out. The Fed paid out 100 cents on the dollar to Goldman Sachs, Societe and other banks. See Wikipedia: "Maiden Lane". It is possible that without these payouts, these banks may have failed or been in very weak conditions. Reportedly, one of the tricks used by European banks was to reduce their capital requirements by getting something off the Balance Sheet by covering it with CDS (i.e., the risk is cancelled out so why do we need 8% capital for it). Of course, if AIG failed, their CDS insurance was worth nothing. This could have been a factor in the Fed bailout (i.e., saving European banks from possible failure and preventing the spread of a worldwide financial Panic).

9-4 $30 Trillion Sham. If there is anyone who believes that the issuers of $30 Trillion of CDS insurance can meet 100% of those claims, I would like to sell you the Brooklyn Bridge. My guess is that maybe there is $0.3 Trillion available to pay claims at the best. To get the idea of the inadequate Capital behind insurance promises, please read Wikipedia: "Monolines". This illustrates how $3 Trillion of municipal bond insurance is being covered by only $0.030 Trillion in Capital. If California defaults on its municipal bonds, there would be no insurance money left to pay the other $2.970 Trillion in municipal bonds.

9-5 Insurance knowledge and "insurable interest". I probably know more about insurance than most of the people selling CDS insurance on Wall St. I was a licensed insurance agent for Life, Health, Property and Casualty. I understand "insurable interest".

9-6 Goldman Sachs Abacus CDO case. Just do a google search to find the details.

9-7 Paulson and no "insurable interest". If Paulson had received an insurance pay out on the fire insurance of a house he did not own, on the other hand, it certainly would have been illegal.

10-1 Never have so few. The "so few" are the people of the relatively small AIG Financial Products group. The "so much" is the $180 Billion lost. The "so many" are the taxpayers that paid for the $180 Billion lost.

11-1 Fed and Wall St. Panic. Some argue that the Fed caused the Panic by a prolonged period of low interest rates. I will agree that this did help create an asset bubble, but it did not cause a Panic. A Panic is something that happens quickly. In my opinion, the flawed Wall St. System deserves credit for that.

11-2 Fed/Treasury. Simplifying the actions of both to just the Fed is definitely a simplification. Secretary of Treasury Paulson probably played a bigger role in letting Lehman go bankrupt than Fed Chief Bernanke, but I want to emphasize lack of Failure Analysis done. I think the Fed with its 21,000 members is the logical place for this activity.

12-1 Uptick Rule. See 7-1 above.

12-2 FICO. See 6-1 above.

13-1 Short Selling. This is betting that a stock will go down in price and is beyond the scope of this book.

14-1 About $400 Trillion of the $600 Trillion are interest rate swaps. There is a floating interest rate end and a fixed interest end. The problem comes when interest rates spike upwards, and the floating end gets massacred as Orange County did in 1994 with its floating rate notes (see Wikipedia: Robert Citron). Recently, Greek 2 year bonds spiked from 5% to 20% before EU intervention. This type of interest spiking could cause a Panic that would make Subprimes look tame.

16-1 Black Swan. See Appendix 10. "Black Swans and Bad Inputs"

Appendix 1. Increasing Homeownership Responsibly

The Subprime Mortgage program has turned into one of the true financial disasters in history. The motivation was OK, but that was about it. How do we expand homeownership to low income, poor credit borrowers? I'm going to put my Financial Planner hat on and show how. The bottomline is this. We don't give these people a house for zero downpayment. We have them do it the old fashioned way by "earning it".

A Typical Subprime Buyer

I am just amazed to read that the $75 Billion program to help save Subprime Buyers has as its aim to reduce their payments to 40% of their income. Let me use that as a starting point and show why this isn't viable. And if they are "reducing" payments to only 40%, what does this mean? Were they at 50%????

Let's start with a $200,000 house and a Subprime Buyer with an income of $30,000 paying a teaser rate of 6% or 0.06 on his mortgage. Namely, $200,000 x 0.06 = $12,000/year. A subtotal for all Housing Related Expenses (Mortgage, Property Tax etc.) and an estimate for the remaining Living Costs (Food, Car etc.) is shown below:

Housing Related Expenses
	$12,000	Mortgage
	$ 2,000	Property Tax
	$ 2,000	Utilities (elec, gas, water, trash)
Subtotal	$16,000	

Other Living Costs
	$6,000	Food (pretty skinny)
	$4,000	Car(s); payments, gas, insurance
	$1,000	Taxes (State and Federal)
	$3,000	Misc: clothes, cellphone, misc
Subtotal	$14,000	

The Subprime Buyer barely makes it.

	$16,000	Housing
	$14,000	Living
Total	$30,000	this matches his income

However, when the teaser rate period ends and the mortgage goes up to 8% to reflect his risk, the mortgage payments go up from $12,000 to $16,000 driving his costs up to $34,000 which exceeds his income. No one should wonder why we have such a horrendous Subprime failure rate. How irresponsible for lenders to make these loans, Fannie and Freddie to buy them and Congress to push them.

My Responsible Program
Rather than having the mortgage lender foreclose on the Subprime Buyer and recognize a huge $40,000 loss, I propose that the lender turn the Subprime Buyer into a Subprime Renter. Let's say rents are 4.5% of the value of the property (0.045 x $200,000 = $9,000). Now if I keep all the other costs the same, I have:

Housing Related Costs
$9,000 Rent
$ 0 Property Tax
$2,000 Utilities
Subtotal $11,000 instead of the $16,000
Living Subtotal $14,000 remains the same
Total $25,000 which means $5,000 savings

Now after 2 years of savings, the Subprime Buyer has $10,000 in the bank. Does he go out and buy a $200,000 house which he can barely make assuming nothing goes wrong? No, he buys a $150,000 house which gives him some margin of safety. He put 5% (or $7,500) down and keeps $2,500 as a cash reserve (Financial Planners always insist on a cash reserve). Mortgage costs are: $150,000 x 0.06 = $9,000. This is the same as his rent so his total costs are $26,500 (as an owner he has to pay $1,500 property tax that he didn't have to do as a renter). The buyer is buying slightly below his income of $30,000/year so he has some margin of $3,500/year.

Living within your income (with margin)
Now in this age of instant gratification, it might seem unreasonable to ask a Subprime Buyer to buy a smaller $150,000 home. Why, this might even mean a 2 bedroom, 1 bath house. (Although, if you look at realtors.com, $150K will get you a 5 bed 3 bath house in Las Vegas).

My wife and I actually have some experience with a family of four living in a 2 bed, 1 bath house/apartment. My wife lived her entire childhood in a 2 bed, 1 bath apartment. I lived half my childhood in a 2 bed, 1 bath house. My mother lived in a 1 bed, 1 bath house as a member of a household of 5 people. It can be done, and it won't leave lasting damage on the family. In my mother's case, she became a Registered Nurse, one brother went through Annapolis and retired as a Navy Commander. The other brother retired as a Vice President of Texas Instruments. And their 1 bed, 1 bath house was only 600 square feet. My mother and her Mom slept in the bedroom, and the father and two boys slept in the living room. Subprime Buyers that have to start out in a basic 2 bed, 1 bath house and cry about it will get no sympathy from this quarter.

Downpayments in Europe

Europe has not had nearly the foreclosure rate on houses as the US has. Why? One of the prime reasons is that in Europe they actually require a downpayment. Generally, the downpayment is 20%. Based on the data in Wikipedia: "Subprime Mortgage Crisis" (see mortgage market), it appears that approximately 8 million homeowners have been foreclosed on or are in the foreclosure process. We should get the statistics on how many of these foreclosures are from zero downpayment buyers. My guess is that it is about 6 million or 75% of the foreclosures. That's just a guess. Whatever the number is, I am sure it is in the millions. If even a 5% downpayment had been required, probably the major part of our Subprime disaster and housing disaster could have been avoided. While I don't admire the European economic model, it is clear that their emphasis on downpayments is sound.

The $75 Billion Subprime Bailout Program

The objective of using this $75 Billion of taxpayer money is to bailout Subprime buyers and help them stay in their homes. It's not working. Perhaps a few hundred thousand of the approximately 10 million Subprime buyers have been helped. A better approach would have been to simply reimburse them their downpayment as much as possible. If every Subprime buyer put down 5% and purchased a $200,000 house, this would total $100 Billion ($10K x 10 million = $100 Bil). Obviously, $75 Billion could have reimbursed 10 million buyers $7,500 of their $10,000 downpayment. Instead of 10 million being helped only a few hundred thousand will be helped since the money is going towards paying down the mortgages. Dumb plan. Please read Appendix 2 because I doubt if most Subprime buyers put money down.

Appendix 2. Why NINJA buyers can't lose

There is a great deal of moaning and groaning about Subprime buyers losing their houses. What is not pointed out is that the Subprime buyers who put no money down can't lose any money. Figure 7.2 showed a normal downpayment buyer's Balance Sheet as Case 1. Let's update that for a "zero downpayment" buyer as shown below:

Balance Sheet for "Zero Downpayment" Buyers – Case 1	
Assets	**Debt**
$200,000	**$200,000**
	Capital
	0
Total $200,000	**$200,000**

Notice that the difference from Figure 7.2 is that the Capital is now zero (no downpayment) and the Debt is equal to the Asset at $200,000. Figure 7.6 showed how the Capital varied when the Asset value was 200, 400, 160. Recall that $200,000 was shortened to 200. If I update Guido's Vertical Balance Sheet (Fig 7.6) for a Subprime borrower putting no money down, the Debt will be constant at 200 and the Capital will vary as the Asset value changes. However, I have to add another line for Bank Losses as shown in the Figure below:

Guido's Vertical Balance Sheet for Cases 1,2,3 Subprime			
	Case 1	Case 2	Case 3
Assets	200	400	160
- Debt	200	200	200
Capital	0	200	0
Bank Loss	0	0	(40)

Case 1 shows no Capital since there was no downpayment. Case 2 shows a nice $200,000 profit since the Asset value went up. Case 3 shows a ($40,000) loss but not for the Subprime borrower. Since he put no money down, the bank suffers the loss.

Despite not losing any money, there is a $75 Billion program (all taxpayer money) to help save Subprime buyers. This is utter nonsense. The zero downpayment buyers had no money to lose. Essentially they were just Renters who also make no downpayment. However, unlike Renters, they could make money if the value of their house went up.

Appendix 3. CFTC Regulation

The CFTC regulates one type of Derivative – Futures. An example of a Futures Contract was given in Example 2 (Chapter 8) where an Airline is using a Futures Contract to guard against the price of oil rising above $80/barrel. The first characteristic to note about a Futures Contract is that it is traded publicly on an exchange, usually on a daily basis. This makes sure that the contract is not opaque. In other words, everyone can look in the newspaper or access the data on a computer screen and see what the price of the contract is. It is not a secret.

The second important characteristic of a Futures Contract is that it is settled on a daily basis. In other words, if on one day the price of oil goes up from $80 to $85, the seller of the Futures Contract must put $5 in an escrow account. If the price goes up to $89 on the next day, the seller must put an additional $4 in the escrow account. This gives the Futures Contract credibility. In Chapter 9, Credit Default Swaps (CDS) will be discussed. The CDS issued by AIG had no credibility. When it came time to pay out on a CDS claim or put up collateral, AIG was shown to not have nearly enough money. We taxpayers have ended up bailing out AIG CDS to the tune of $180 Billion. If this AIG CDS had been regulated by the CFTC, this never would have happened. As soon as AIG could not settle up on a daily basis, everyone would have seen that AIG CDS had no further credibility. Instead, we received a gigantic $180 Billion surprise.

While I think the CFTC type of regulation is a vast improvement over no regulation, I think it has a flaw that should be addressed. Let's go back to the seller of the Oil Future Contract at $80. Let's say that the Persian Gulf is closed due to war, and the price of oil jumps to $200/barrel. Let's say the issuer of the Futures Contract runs out of money when oil reaches a price of $150. Obviously the contract will be over at that point, but shouldn't the Airline have been given that information at the start? For example, it would have been more honest and complete if the seller had agreed to sell a Futures contract for oil at $80/barrel and guarantee payment up to $150/barrel and no further. As it stands now, the seller guarantees an infinite price which is not realistic.

In summary, the CFTC regulates its Futures Derivatives well. The information is public. The settlements are daily. CFTC regulation does not slow down Futures sales. The CFTC is a model for limited, intelligent regulation.

Appendix 4. Complexity of Derivatives

Each layer or tranche of a Mortgage Derivative (as shown in Figures 8.2 & 8.3) could be sold individually as a CDO Derivative. These CDO Derivatives could be purely made up from a Subprime Mortgage Pool or a normal Mortgage Pool or a mix of the two types of Mortgages. Additionally, these individual CDOs could be mixed together to make a giant CDO. For example, a single CDO could be made up from a pool of 1,000 mortgages. A giant CDO could be made up of 10 individual CDOs or ultimately have a pool of 10,000 mortgages. Now how hard do you think it would be to analyze the value of this CDO of CDOs? It would be nearly impossible which is why they were described as opaque.

The complexity was even worse than this. The mortgage pools could be made up of different types of mortgages such as: fixed rate, interest only, negative amortization and variable rates. Now it is not necessary to understand what these different types of mortgages are. What is important to understand is that it was such a mish mash no one could truly evaluate the worth of any pool or Derivative.

Let me just illustrate this with just one type of Subprime Mortgage known as the 2/28. This meant that the mortgage was fixed for 2 years at some rate, say 5%. After the 2 year period, the mortgage rate varied depending upon some interest rate index such as the LIBOR (London Inter Bank Offer Rate). A typical variable rate might be the index rate + 4 %. If the index rate is 6%, then the variable rate is 6 + 4 = 10%. The poor Subprime Mortgage holder will see his monthly payments double when the variable rate starts. This is known as the reset point, and is the point at which many Subprimes failed. If the underlying index interest rate dropped to 5% during the next year, the Subprime rate would change to 5 + 4 = 9%. Now can you see the difficulty in determining the value of 10,000 mortgages when many of them have variable rates (different variable rates)? It was a total mess.

The real damage that this complexity brought to the market is that some Subprimes were mixed in with normal mortgages. Thus, no one could be sure if any real estate Derivative was safe. Irrationally, this fear extended to Commercial Real Estate and other types of Derivatives creating a fearful $5 Trillion Toxic Monster. The problem that Wall St. faced was closer to a $200 Billion problem. See Appendix 5.

Appendix 5. Size of Subprimes

5.1 Size of Subprimes and their Losses

I have estimated the size of the US real estate mortgage market at $10 Trillion with the Subprimes at $2 Trillion. This is what I based my estimates on when I wrote my Letters to the Editor to financial publications in October of 2008. Where did these numbers come from?

Well, I knew that the number of real estate sales each year was between 6 to 7 million. To be conservative, I estimated that the Subprime sales were 5 million in each of the two years of the worst NINJA loans (roughly 2005 and 2006). This gave me a nice round number of 10 million. Now since I also knew that the average price of a US house was $200,000, it was a simple matter of multiplying $200,000 x 10 million to get $2 Trillion in Subprime loans.

Please look at Wikipedia: "Subprime Loan Crisis". If you read the estimate of this article, their numbers are $1.3 Trillion in Subprime Loans with 7.5 million Subprime borrowers. This is less that my estimates of $2 Trillion and 10 million borrowers which means the losses were less than my estimates (not the $5 Trillion Toxic Monster of Wall St.).

Now in this Wikipedia article, they estimate the Subprime Losses through August 2008 as $500 Billion for financial institutions worldwide. This is in line with my prediction. I assumed a 20% of $2 Trillion which is $400 Billion. If the world (mostly Europe) received the other $100 Billion, then we are in agreement. Now I want to make one very important point that the Wikipedia article doesn't make. It just talks about "financial institutions" in one giant lump. I think it is very important to separate Wall St. from Fannie Mae and Freddie Mac. Since Fannie/Freddie holds $5 Trillion of the total $10 Trillion in mortgages, I made the simple split of 50/50 for the losses. Half the $400 Billion loss would go to Fannie/Freddie and half to Wall St. Now in September 2008, the Fed bailed out Fannie/Freddie with $180 Billion. This roughly checks with the $200 Billion loss I projected for them. Therefore this gives some credence to my projection of a $200 Billion Subprime Loss for Wall St.

In fact, if you read the book, "Subprime Mortgage Credit Derivatives' by Goodman et. al., their estimate is closer to a 2/3 split for Fannie/Freddie and 1/3 for Wall St. This means the Wall St. Subprime

Loss might even be less than $200 Billion. It might be more like $120 Billion.

Now, the Wikipedia article says that by November of 2008, that $750 Billion of Subprime Losses had been recognized. This doesn't mean that they all failed, but it means they were projected to fail. Again, if we split between the US, and the rest of the world, the US might be left with $600 Billion in losses. Using a 50/50 split, this would be the high estimate in my Tables shown in Appendix 8. "Bank Capital and Subprime Losses". Wall St. would have be hit with $300 Billion in Losses. This would be worse, but Wall St. would have survived with its $800 Billion in capital. If the $300 Billion number is right, then probably Morgan Stanley would have been in trouble. As it was, it received a cash infusion from the Japanese and TARP.

Remember also that my Tables in Appendix 7. "Bank Capital and Subprime Losses" apportion all the Subprime Loss only to the most vulnerable investment banks. This wasn't the true case. Some of the normal banks had Subprime Losses as well. This would have taken some of the load off the investment banks. Furthermore, some of the Subprime losses were taken by other banks such as Countrywide, Indymac, Wachovia, Washington Mutual and others (as shown in Table 11.1).

My point is this. The losses that Wall St. banks faced were somewhere in the $80 to $300 Billion range. Their $800 Billion in capital was able to take this blow. There was no reason for Panic.

Subprime Failure Rate
Let's assume that the Wikipedia numbers of $1.3 Trillion in Subprime Mortgages and $750 Billion in Subprime Losses (actual or projected by Nov 2008) are right. What does this say about the Subprime Failure rate? Well 750/1,300 = 0.57. ***That's a 57% failure rate!!!*** Now remember normal mortgages fail at a 2% failure rate. This Congressionally sponsored program has to be the worst in history. You're paying for it. Furthermore, the Wikipedia article projects $1.5 Trillion of Subprimes to fail. Well, there is a little inconsistency here, because they had earlier stated that there were $1.3 Trillion of Subprimes. Nevertheless, they are projecting something like a 100% failure rate.

5.2 Subprime Models

Now let me make another observation. The issuers of Subprime Mortgage Backed Securities made math models projecting their performance and therefore their value. Do you think they used 57% failure rates in those models??? Do you think the Rating Agencies used 57% failure rates in their models which earned these Derivatives a AAA rating??? If I sound a little condescending, maybe you can start to figure out why. See Appendix 6 for a further discussion of the math modeling behind Subprime Derivative construction and their evaluation by Rating Agencies.

5.3 Disclosure of Information

Don't you think it would be in the public interest to know how many Subprimes were generated (e.g., by year) and how many have failed. Do you think the Dept of Housing and Urban Affairs (HUD) knows? They keep meticulous statistics on housing. Do you think the Fed and Treasury know? I think they all do. Why can we not find this information anywhere but Wikipedia? Is it because it is being politically hushed up?

5.4 Subprime Failures Left

Again, based on the foreclosure table shown in Wikipedia, roughly 8 million foreclosures have occurred or are in process. Let's assume 6 million of them are Subprimes. Since there were only 7.5 Subprimes to begin with, this would leave at most 1.5 million left to fail. Perhaps some can survive. If not, the remaining failures should occur in 2010. Once this Subprime poison is out of the system, a normal housing recovery can take place.

Appendix 6. Derivative Math Models

This Appendix is purely optional because it may be too detailed for some readers. I am going to give some explanation why the modeling for the Mortgage Backed Derivatives turned out to be so flawed. The values of these Derivatives were determined by complex computer models. I will briefly discuss just two problems with these models: (1) the formulas are only good for small perturbations (changes) and (2) the formulas were derived from improper data.

Recommendation: Analyze the Math Models
Math Models are part of the basis for the formation of Derivatives, CDS and the Ratings put out by the Rating Agencies. An independent, competent authority should examine these models and their inputs. I don't think the SEC is up to the task of analyzing Derivatives, but I bet some good mathematicians could make both Derivative makers and Rating Agencies squirm.

Garbage in and Garbage out
"Garbage in and Garbage out" is a familiar saying in the world of computer programming. What it means is that you can have the greatest computer program (or computer model) in the world, but, if you feed in bad data, you will get bad results. The computer models designed for valuing Derivatives suffered from a similar problem.

Problem (1) Models good for only small perturbations (changes)
Let's assume for the moment the Derivative Value Models are valid for small failure rates such as the 2% failure rate of normal Mortgages. Then, if real data with only a 2% failure rate was fed into the model, the output results would be valid. In fact, the model still might work up to perhaps a 7% failure rate. However, if that input data was changed to a 20% failure rate (e.g., Subprimes) the model would just blow up. This is what I suspect was part of the problem with the Mortgage Derivative computer models. The computer models were designed for normal Mortgages, the input failure rate for Subprimes was assumed to be too low (e.g., 7%) and the model gave a reassuring value for the Derivative. In fact, if the true failure rate of Subprimes (e.g., 20% or higher) was input to the model, it would have just blown up.

Now I am not privy to the models used by the Derivative makers or the Rating Agencies that evaluated these Derivatives and gave them a rating like AAA, but if some competent math team could get their hands on these models and the input data used (assumed failure rates), the team could then test them against the real data (actual failure rates). My guess is that with 20% failure rate data fed into these models, the models would blow up (i.e., give no value to the Derivative). What this means is that the Derivative never should have been made or marketed in the first place. It means the Rating Agencies should never have given such a Derivative a AAA rating.

When I describe problem (1) as small perturbations (changes), I mean that the model might handle 2 to 7% failure rates but not a 20% failure rate.

Problem (2) Bad Model made from improper/insufficient data
For the sake of the above discussion, I assumed that the models were OK and just broke down under when high failure rate data was input. However, I suspect that the models weren't that good. Basically, these models were derived from curve fitting data. In other words, you have a bunch of data points (e.g., failure rates) over time and fit a curve through them. For example, life insurance companies have 100 years of data on what percentage of people die at a given age and can price (value) their life insurance accordingly. A 20 year old is going to pay less than a 60 year old. The life insurance companies have good models because they have lots of data.

Now perhaps there are 50 years of data for normal mortgages. Then a pretty good curve (or model) could be developed for this data.

However, there was not 50 years of data on the no downpayment NINJA loans that started hitting the system in 2005 – 2007. If a Derivative was made in 2006 with these NINJA Subprimes, there might have been 1 year of data available. Furthermore, many of these Subprime loans were known as 2/28. This meant they had a 2 year fixed rate (perhaps at a teaser rate low level of interest) and then the next 28 years of the mortgage would be at a variable rate which was almost inevitably much higher. The end of the 2 year point was the reset point where so many Subprimes failed. Therefore a 2005 Subprime would not start failing at its reset point until 2007. A model of these Subprimes made before 2007 was made without taking the reset point into account.

Problems (1) and (2)
What I have tried to sketch out here is that the Derivative Makers and Rating Agencies probably suffered from both bad models and real

world input data with much higher failure rates that they ever expected. They thought they were dealing with good data like what was available to the life insurance companies or available from normal mortgages. They didn't realize they were dealing with insufficient data on Subprimes.

Predictive Capability

Now if you are a scientist and have a theory, the acid test is how well does that theory predict some future event. My theory is that the Derivative Makers and the people *selling* CDS insurance (next Chapter) on these Derivatives had bad models. Well, if you knew this, you could *buy* the CDS insurance on these Derivatives and make a killing. This is exactly what John Paulson did as described in the book, "The Greatest Trade Ever" by Gregory Zuckerman. If you read the book carefully, you will find that the first thing he did was gather a lot of mortgage data. Then he looked for the parameters that correlated with failure. When he found out that the CDS sellers had missed these parameters in their models, he knew that they had priced their CDS insurance way too low (essentially the CDS sellers never expected any failures). He bought $Millions of CDS from these suckers, and, when the Derivatives failed, they had to pay him off at 100 to 1 (the price of insurance was only 1% of the pay off amount). He made $20 Billion. He made $1 Billion in the now famous Goldman Abacus CDO. I don't admire him for making money while contributing no value added, but I will say that he did his math homework unlike the Derivative makers and Rating Agencies.

Derivative, CDS Models and Rocket Science

The people that come up with the models for Derivatives and CDS are called "Quants". This is short for Quantitative Analyst. Frequently, they are mathematicians and physicists (my kind of people). Are they stupid? No. Do they and their models appear to be nearly infallible to the managers, MBAs and stock brokers at their banks? Yes. Very few of the managers, MBAs and brokers have much of a math background at all. Consequently, they are extremely dependent on these "Rocket Scientists".

Perhaps an analogy is this. Let's say that you can only speak one word of French, "Merci". I can speak 20 sentences in French. That's enough for me to snow you. I could tell you that I spoke fluent French. You would never know that I didn't. You have no way of checking. Now, if you had a friend that spoke fluent French, that person could do a thorough job of checking out my fluency. This is why I recommend a independent math-competent team be used to check the Derivative and CDS models as well as their input data.

If the bank managers are in no position to evaluate the quality of these models, Regulators are in even worse shape. They are lawyer heavy organizations, and lawyers don't have a lot of math in their curriculum. What the Regulators need to do is beef up their organizations with some "Quants" (or borrow someone from the NTSB). Now one of the problems the Derivatives and CDS discussed in this book is that they weren't regulated at all. However, if they were regulated with the existing Regulatory organization, it is likely that the mathematical models wouldn't have been examined at all.

Rocket Science and Wall St. Models
I want to make a final comment on Wall St.'s "Rocket Science". Are these models "Rocket Science"? No. "Rocket Science" is what was done by the aerospace industry, and it is several levels above what Wall St. is doing. Much of the Wall St. modeling is based on statistics which is at the bottom of the math food chain. Now more math than that is used including present value, probability and even a partial differential equation for the Black Sholes Theorem. However, this really can't be called "Rocket Science". To get an idea of what "Rocket Science" is, take a look at "Elements of Gas Dynamics" by Lipmann and Roshko or "Re-entry and Planetary Entry" by Loh. These books have hundreds of equations just a little more complex than the Black Sholes Theorem. (And once I even understood them.)

Appendix 7. Turning Subprimes into AAA

The Goldman Sachs Abacus CDO is an example of how some Subprime Mortgages were magically turned into AAA quality CDOs. This is the equivalent of a taking a bunch of D students and turning a couple of them into A students. Here is the process using students as an example:

1. I start with 10 "D" students who score 60% of their exam which I just represent as 6. Thus the combined score for the 10 students is simply 10 (students) x 6 (score) = 60. Now before my teaching performance is reviewed by the Principal, I show the results to the Vice Principal. He is dismayed that all I can produce is D students. He asks if I can't produce just 1 or 2 A students.

2. Before I see the Principal, I decide I need to take action. The Principal will only see the total score from the class and not the distribution. Now, as a completely unethical teacher, I redistribute the scores to make 2 "A" students (score = 9), 1 B student (score = 8), 1 C student (score = 7), 3 F students (score = 5) and 3 F students (score =4) for a total score of 60.

3. Unfortunately for me half my original set of D students fail the next test completely and get a score of zero (5 x 0 = 0). Half still get a D score of 6 (5 x 6 = 30). I still want to keep my A students so I distribute the scores: 2 A students (score = 9), 1 B student (score = 8), 1 F student (score = 4) and 6 F students (score = 0) for a total score of 30.

4. The Derivative shown in Figure 8.2 has only three layers. In reality, Derivatives may have had 10 layers. Since the lower layers were going to take all the losses (as with the F students above), the top layers could be rated as AAA because the models predicted only low loss rates (say 10% or less). In fact, when the losses were something like 50%, many of the upper layers were affected as well.

The moral to this story is that it is about as tough to turn D students into A students as it is to turn Subprimes into AAA quality mortgages. The ethics involved is about the same.

Appendix 8. Bank Capital and Subprime Losses

If there were $200 Billion in Subprime Losses absorbed by Wall St., why was it that Bear and Lehman failed vs. other banks. The answer is Financial Cause (1) Balance Sheet Abuse.

Estimate of Wall St. Capital And Subprime Losses (2008)			
Normal Bank (8% Cap)	Capital ($ Bil)	Subprime Loss ($ Bil)	Net
JP Morgan	174	0	174
Bank of America	177	0	177
Wells Fargo	125	0	125
Citi	141	0	141
NY Mellon	27	0	27
Subtotal	644	0	644
Investment Banks (2% Cap)			
Goldman Sachs	64	40	24
Morgan Stanley	50	40	10
Merrill Lynch	30	40	(10)
Lehman Brothers	16	40	(24)
Bear Stearns	10	40	(30)
Subtotal	170	200	(30)
Total	814	200	614

In the Table above, I show the Capitalization (or Capital) of the 10 largest Wall St. banks. The top 5 Normal Banks had approximately 8% capitalization while the lower 5 Investment Banks had approximately 2% capitalization. Obviously, the Investment Banks had less Capital to cushion any losses. Therefore in the second column, I distribute the $200 Billion in Subprime Losses just to the 5 Investment Banks. The numbers in the "Net" column are arrived at by subtracting the Subprime Losses in column 2 from the Bank Capital in column 1. What's left is the net capital (+ or -).

Example. Net for Bear
The Capital for Bear was $10 Billion. The Subprime Loss I allocated was $40 Billion. The "Net" was $(30) Billion as determined from $10 Bil - $40 Bil = -$30 Bil or $(30) Bil.

Now do we know exactly how the Subprime Losses were distributed between the Wall St. Banks? No. That's a secret. In order to make a Ball Park estimate, I just equally apportioned the $200 Billion between the 5 Investment Banks. How does this Ball Park estimate correspond to reality? Well, Bear was taken over by JP Morgan "after" it received $30 Billion from the Fed. While $30 Billion may not have been the Bear loss, it does look like it was in the neighborhood. Lehman went bankrupt, and we may get a number when that is all over. All the talk on the weekend that the Treasury/Fed were trying to orchestrate a Lehman takeover was that there was a $30 Billion hole on its Balance Sheet. This is in the neighborhood of my $(24) Billion estimate. Merrill Lynch, of course, was taken over by Bank of America on that same weekend, but later returned to the Fed for $30 Billion to cover the takeover. This suggests that the Merrill loss was bigger than my estimate of $(10) Billion. While my estimates may not be exact, they seem to be in the Ball Park.

Sensitivity Analysis
Well, one might argue that my estimate for Subprime Losses seen by Wall St. may have been different than $200 Billion. What if they were lower at $100 Billion or even higher at $300 Billion. Would the results be any different? Would all the banks have failed? In the engineering world, we call this type checking a "Sensitivity Analysis", and it is shown in the next Table. Only the Investment Banks are shown since they were the most vulnerable. The first table just compares the Bank Capital with Subprime Low ($100/5 = 20), Subprime Best ($200/5 = 40) and Subprime High ($300/5 = 60).

Estimate of Wall St. Capitalization And Subprime Losses (in $ Bil)				
Investment		Subprime Loss Estimate		
Bank	Capitalization	Low	Best	High
Goldman Sachs	64	20	40	60
Morgan Stanley	50	20	40	60
Merrill Lynch	30	20	40	60
Lehman	16	20	40	60
Bear	10	20	40	60
Total	170	100	200	300

The Table below just does the Net process for all three columns – Low, Best and High. What the results generally show is that Bear, Lehman and Merrill were in trouble for both the low through high estimates. In other words, these Investment Banks were "insensitive" to the Subprime Loss estimate whether it was $100, 200 or 300 Billion.

Investment	Estimate of Wall St. Capitalization After subtracting Subprime Losses (in $ Bil)			
		Net Capital		
Bank	Capitalization	Low	Best	High
Goldman Sachs	64	44	24	4
Morgan Stanley	50	30	10	(10)
Merrill Lynch	30	10	(10)	(30)
Lehman	16	(4)	(24)	(44)
Bear	10	(10)	(30)	(50)

Now, of course, the above Table shows Morgan Stanley in trouble in the High case and Merrill OK in the Low case. But what I am trying to show at a Magic +1 level is that 3 Investment Banks were in trouble. All of the Wall St. Banks weren't. There was no necessity for Panic, for the TARP or for the Stimulus Package. What we needed at this critical point in time was great leadership, and we didn't get it.

In Chapter 11 (Table 11.1), I show an estimate for the Subprime Losses already written down by Wall St. I estimated $120 Billion. This would correspond most closely to the $100 Billion loss described above as the Low estimate for the Subprime Losses.

Until the Fed, HUD and Wall St. truly define what the Subprime Losses were, we will all have to make estimates. This Appendix has shown the impact of Low ($100 Billion) to High ($300 Billion) on the Wall St. Banks. The answer is generally that 3 Investment Banks were in trouble, and the rest of Wall St. would have survived. Remember that you must multiply my Low and High estimates by 2 to get the whole Subprime Loss because I estimate that half went to Fannie and Freddie.

Appendix 9. The Rule of 72

I'm trying to keep the discussion on Derivatives as simple as possible. In Chapter 8, I introduce the layering or tranching concept of these Derivatives. The 1st layer gets the first 10% of the losses for the entire pool and is then wiped out. Why would anyone want to buy this layer or tranche? The reason is that there is potentially greater gain. The 1st layer might get paid a return of 15% per year. The second layer might get a 10% return, and the relatively safe 3rd layer might get a 5% return.

Now these rates of return are just numbers. Another way of looking at is to ask the question, "How long does it take me to double my money?" In other words, "How long does it take me to double my money at a 15% rate of return vs. a 5% rate of return?"

One of the techniques used by Financial Planners is called the "Rule of 72". It is pretty simple. What you do is divided the rate of return into 72, and the answer is a good approximation of how many years it takes to double your money.

Example: "How long does it take me to double my money if I earn a rate of return of 15%?" If I divide 72 by 15, I get approximately 5 years.

Compare that to a rate of return of 5%. If I divide 72 by 5, I get approximately 15 years. Well, if I want to make a lot of money quickly, I will definitely take the 15% rate of return layer......if I don't worry about risk.

Appendix 10. Black Swans and Bad Inputs

This whole book is concerned with a flawed Wall St. System. In other words, if another Bad Input other than Subprimes comes along, it could also cause a Panic and a Crash. That is why it is so important to fix the flaws in the Wall St. System. Well, one might ask, "What are some other examples of Bad Inputs? I will give a short sketch of some past and possible future Bad Inputs. In the engineering world, we call a bad input to a system simply a Bad Input. However, in the financial world, they use a more elegant term – a Black Swan Event.

Black Swan Event
Seeing a Black Swan is rare. This term is used to describe some event that might only happen once in 10,000 years. This is how LTCM strategized its trading. Unfortunately, a Black Swan (Bad Input) in the form of a Russian Default ruined their plan. Subprimes were another Black Swan. It turns out these Black Swans are not really so rare.

Some Black Swans in the Past.
In 1998, the Russian Debt Default (Black Swan) nearly caused a market collapse when the large Hedge Fund, LTCM, nearly folded. A last minute rescue by a consortium of Wall St. Banks prevented market chaos.

In 1987, the stock market dropped 25% in one day due to programmed trading or portfolio management.

On 9/11/2001, terrorists crashed planes into the World Trade Center necessitating deep interest rate cuts by the Fed to save the market.

On May 6, 2010, the Dow dropped 10% in 15 minutes. Accenture, a major stock, dropped from $40/share to 1 cent per share. The SEC hasn't figured out why yet, but my guess is that it is the ultra fast programmed trading by Hedge Funds.

Some Possible Future Black Swans.
Greece is probably going to default on its debt. Just before it received a temporary rescue by the Eurozone, the interest rate on its 2 year bonds spiked from 5% to 20% in one day. If Greece defaults on its debt, we are likely to see more such interest rate spikes on a variety of European

bonds. Who cares? The people holding the floating end of some of the mind boggling $400 Trillion of interest rate swaps (Derivatives) will care. What will happen to them will be similar to what happened to Orange County, California when it went bankrupt because it held the wrong end of an interest rate Derivatives. For a discussion of the Orange County bankruptcy see Wikipedia: "Robert Citron" (the controller for Orange County).

The Euro could wobble or collapse due to problems with the other debt and deficit endangered Eurozone nations (Portugal, Italy, Ireland, Greece, Spain known as the PIIGS). Interest rates could go up, and the holders of the wrong end of interest rate Derivatives could get massacred. This is why it is essential to separate Banks from Derivatives (the Volcker Rule).

Israel could attack the nuclear bomb program of Iran. In response, the Iranians could close the Strait of Hormuz and therefore shut down 40% of the world's tradable oil which would result in the price of oil doubling in 4 to 6 weeks. This price increase could ruin car companies, airlines and more as happened in 1973.

My point is this. Black Swans aren't that rare. They show up all the time. We must have a financial system that can weather the storm. It didn't weather the Subprime storm. We need to make changes. Having $600 Trillion of Derivatives and $30 Trillion of CDS is just financial insanity. We have to change this or suffer another Panic.

Well, one might argue that if I am so sure that $600 Trillion in unregulated Derivatives is dangerous, why haven't we had another Panic? My answer is that it takes the right Black Swan to cause a particular type of failure and Panic. The Subprime Black Swan caused the Subprime Derivatives to fail. The effects of a Greek Default Black Swan could cause a good portion of the $400 Trillion of Interest Rate Derivatives to fail. The Black Swans are out there. It is just a matter of time before another one swims into view.

Bibliography

"A Demon of our own Design", R. Bookstaber
A good book on Hedge Funds and the crash of 1987.

"All About Derivatives", Michael Durbin
A good first primer on Derivatives with formulas.

"A Colossal Failure of Common Sense", L. MacDonald
The failure of Lehman Brothers.

"Capitalism, Socialism and Democracy", Schumpeter
Why Capitalism is best.

"Collateralized Debt Obligations", Lucas et. al.
Detailed discussion of CDO Derivatives.

"Collateralized Debt Obligations", J. Tavakoli
Detailed discussion of CDO Derivatives.

"Credit Derivatives & Synthetic Structures", Tavakoli
Detailed discussion of Credit Derivatives.

"Den of Thieves", J. Stewart
The story of Drexel, Burnham, Lambert and Michael Milken.

"Electronic Exchanges", Gorham and Singh
Good Chapter on Regulation.

"Fool's Gold", Gillian Tett
How Derivatives began with JP Morgan.

"House of Cards", William Cohan
The failure of Bear Stearns.

"In Fed We Trust", David Wessel
The role of the Fed in the 2008 Panic.

"Last Man Standing", D. MacDonald
The story of Jamie Dimon, head of JP Morgan.

"Liar's Poker", M. Lewis
Details how Wall St. Traders view customers as suckers. The author quit when he realized he was adding no value.

"Mellon", D. Cannadine
The story of the Mellon bank.

"Morgan", J. Stouse
The biography of JP Morgan.

"No one would listen", H. Markopolos
How the SEC failed to investigate Madoff.

"On the Brink", H. Paulson (Sec of Treasury)
His view of the 2008 Panic. He was no JP Morgan.

"Options for the Stock Investor", James Bittman
Explains how options work.

"Quants", S. Patterson
Excellent book on the computerized trading of Hedge Funds.

"Slapped by the Invisible Hand", G. Gorton
Good detailed on Subprime Mortgage Derivatives.

"Subprime Mortgage Credit Derivatives", Goodman
Good study of Subprime Derivatives through 2007.

"The Ascent of Money", N. Ferguson
A review of finance from ancient times until now.

"The Big Short", M. Lewis
How Paulson and others used CDS on securities they didn't own.

"The End of Wall St.", R. Lowenstein
Very good book on the 2008 Panic.

"The Greatest Trade Ever", Gregory Zuckerman
Describes how J. Paulson made $20 Billion with CDS.

"The House of Morgan", R. Chernow
A history of the JP Morgan bank from its origins.

"The House of Rothschild", N. Ferguson
The history of the Rothschild banking empire.

"The Housing Boom", Thomas Sowell
Describes the Subprime Mortgage disaster.

"The Last Partnerships", Charles Geisst
Describes when Investment Banks actually did investing.

"The Road to Serfdom", F. Hayek
Why Capitalism is best.

"The Two Trillion Dollar Meltdown", C. Morris
Good book on the Panic.

"The Wealth of Nations", Adam Smith
Classic book on Capitalism.

"This Time is Different", Reinhart & Rogoff
Eight centuries of financial meltdowns.

"Too Big to Fail", Andrew Sorkin
Good book on the Panic.

"Too Good to be True", E. Arvedlund
The story of the Madoff Ponzi Scheme.

"When Genius Failed", R. Lowenstein

The story of the LTCM hedge fund failure in 1998.

"13 Bankers", S. Johnson and J. Kwak
Very good book details the change from banking to trading and the growth of the largest banks.

DVDs

"The Warning", www.pbs.org
The story of how Brooksley Born tried to regulate Derivatives.

"Thinking About Capitalism", J. Muller
Excellent lectures on capitalism.

"Meaning from Data: Statistics made clear", Starbird
Good primer on statistics.

Websites
www.Wikpedia.com
www.google.com
www.federalreserve.gov
www.bloomberg.com
www.businessweek.com
www.wsj.com (Wall St. Journal)
www.ft.com (Financial Times)

I realize that this is a sizable list of books. My recommendation for the best single book on the 2008 Panic is "The End of Wall St." (with "13 Bankers" as runner-up). The best on the collapse of Bear Stearns is "House of Cards" and "Colossal Failure of Common Sense" on the collapse of Lehman. On the Fed, the best is "In Fed we Trust". On the Subprimes, it is "The Housing Boom". I wish I could recommend one on AIG, but most of the data is being kept secret so it is tough to write a book. One is needed. On how Hedge Funds are dominating the stock market, read both "Quants" and "A Demon of our own Design". The more you read and understand, the more upset you will become. You will understand why we need to get Wall St. back on track.

Glossary

Alt A Mortgage – This is a mortgage whose quality is between a normal mortgage and a Subprime Mortgage.

ASAP – As Soon As Possible

Asset – on a Balance Sheet, this is something such as a house or cash.

Ball Park Thinking – see Chapter 2

Balance Sheet – see Chapter 5

Belly up – a term used for failure. A dead fish floats belly up.

Black Box – This is not the Black Box searched for when an airplane crashes. In this book, it is an engineering Black Box which is a simplification of a complex system like an electrical system or a financial system.

Bond – see definition in Chapter 7

Capital – On a Balance Sheet, this is the difference between the Assets – Debt. It is also called equity or net worth.

Capitalism – Where the ownership and control of the economy is basically in private hands. The system objective is to add value.

Capitalization – How much capital a company has.

Certified Financial Planner – trained in investment, insurance, taxes, retirement planning and estate planning

Communism – Economically, this is ownership and control of the nation's economy.

Credit Default Swaps – see Chapter 9

Debt – On a Balance Sheet, this is borrowed money owed by the company. Usually this is fixed interest rate bonds. Debt = Liabilities

Default – When a person fails to pay on a mortgage or a company fails to pay on a debt.

Derivative – This is a financial product derived from some underlying asset. Also it could be a condition or index. See Definition in Chapter 8

Equity – also known as capital or net worth. See Capital.

Fannie Mae – along with Freddie Mac, these secondary mortgage market entities hold half US mortgages

Failure – I define this to mean either a default or foreclosure on a Subprime Mortgage.

Fed – the Federal Reserve, the US central bank

Freddie Mac – see Fannie Mae

Foreclosure – If the mortgage borrower fails to make payments for 3 to 4 months, he will lose the property which will be sold.

Futures – a Futures contract depends on some future event before being exercised.

Hedge Funds – These are totally secret, investment funds for the wealthy that get around the 50% margin rule for individuals.

Laissez faire – this refers to a market with little or no regulation. This is generally healthy, but Wall St. has abused this.

Liabilities - = Debt. See Debt.

Mortgage Backed Derivatives – Derivatives that are derived from mortgages.

Mortgage Backed Securities = Mortgage Backed Derivatives

NINJA Loans – these were the worst of the Subprime Loans for people with No Income No Job Assets.

Notional Value – A Life Insurance Policy might have a notational value of $100,000, but you only pay $1,000 a year for it. CDS notational value is similar. However, if the person dies or the entity insured by CDS fails, the total value is due for pay out.

Opaque Derivative – Derivatives that are hard to analyze, hard to value.

Overnight Lending – loans that are only good for one day.

Panic – fear of the unknown which in this book is used to describe a sudden loss of confidence in the stock market and economy.

Recession – a slow downturn in the economy.

Repo – this refers to short term financing.

REIT – Real Estate Invest Trust. See Definition Chap 6.

Reset Point – A Subprime Mortgage has a low fixed rate mortgage for 6 months to 2 years and when that time period ends, the mortgage resets to a variable rate (usually higher).

Securitization – In this book, it is the process of turning a long term mortgage into a bond (REIT) or Derivative.

Subprime Mortgage – a mortgage to a borrower with a marginal credit rating. These mortgages, especially the NINJA loans, may have failure rates from 15 to 50% or even higher.

Teaser Rates – An irresponsible lender could tempt a Subprime Borrower with an artificially low mortgage rate that will be raised later.

Welfare State – Usually 50% of the economy is controlled by the government. Greece is an example.

If you want another source for financial word definitions, try:

www.investorwords.com

Acronyms

AIG – American International Group, a large insurance company

CERN – a major physics research facility in France/Switzerland

CDO – Collateralized Debt Obligation, a Derivative

CDS – Credit Default Swap

CFTC – Commodities Futures Trading Commission, monitors the futures market

CPA – Certified Public Accountant, smart accountants

FDIC – Federal Deposit Insurance Corp, protects deposits at banks

Fed – The Federal Reserve, our central bank

GDP – Gross Domestic Product, measures our nation's yearly income

HP – Hewlett Packard, a major computer/electronics company

HUD – Dept of Housing and Urban Development

IED – Improvised Explosive Device used by terrorists, in this book it refers to Derivatives and CDS

IRS – Internal Revenue Service

LIBOR – London InterBank Offered Rate, a reference interest rate

LTCM – Long Term Capital Management, a hedge fund that failed in 1998 and need a Wall St. bailout; leveraged 100 to 1

MBA – Master's in Business Administration

NASD – National Assoc of Securities Dealers, a good self regulating organization; licenses stock brokers

NINJA – No Income No Jobs Assets, the lowest form of Subprime Loan

REIT – Real Estate Investment Trust; a sensible, regulated manner of doing Securitization (without the big bonuses)

Repo Financing – short term financing longer than overnight

SEC – Security Exchange Commission; perhaps the most incompetent regulatory agency around

TARP – Troubled Assets Recovery Plan; the idea was to buy bad Subprime mortgages from banks, but they were so sliced and diced in Derivatives that this became impossible

Fact Table of Financial Elements (In $Trillions)		
Element	Value before Panic	Value after Panic
I. GDP	14	14
II. National Wealth:		
Stock Market	10	5
Total Real Estate	15	12
Other [4-1]	39	33
National Wealth	64	50
III. Real Estate:		
Total Real Estate Value	15	12
Total Mortgages	10	10
Total Equity (Capital)	5	2
IV. Miscellaneous:		
Subprime Mortgages	2	1.6
Bank Capital	0.8	0.6
TARP		0.7
Stimulus Bill		0.8
V. Size of Derivative Market:		
Total Derivatives	600	599
Total CDS	30	30